Does the Bible require a
belief in 'special creation'?

J H John Peet

DayOne

© Day One Publications 2013
First printed 2013

ISBN 978–1–84625–413–0

British Library Cataloguing in Publication Data available

Published by Day One Publications
Ryelands Road, Leominster, HR6 8NZ
☎ 01568 613 740 FAX 01568 611 473
email—sales@dayone.co.uk
web site—www.dayone.co.uk
North America—email—usasales@dayone.co.uk

Cover design by Rob Jones, Elk Design
Printed and bound by TJ International Ltd. Padstow Cornwall

In this book, John Peet presents a positive and concise defence of young-earth creationism that is easy to read. The book contains clear biblical arguments that show the dangers of theistic evolution and how it is incompatible with evangelical Christianity. In particular, John Peet demonstrates how evolution leads to unbiblical views of Adam, man, God and even salvation. He shows how the whole of Scripture regards Genesis 1–2 as historical, and he has included a very helpful summary table of New Testament references to the first two chapters of Genesis. This book will no doubt help many Christians who want to understand the problems of theistic evolution.

Professor Stuart Burgess
Bristol

Dr John Peet has for many years been greatly respected as a champion of speaking boldly and clearly concerning both the biblical position on creation and the science supporting it. In this book, he unequivocally shows the biblical reasons why keeping to a young-earth creation position is so essential. As he states in the Introduction, 'the purpose of this book is to look at the theological issues arising from the subject [of creation]'. He rightly puts a great emphasis on the authority of Scripture and on man's nature, which cannot be understood without recognizing that he is made in the image of God. Dr Peet goes on to stress the importance of the Fall of Man, since so much wrong thinking comes when we underestimate the extent of the Fall. As a summary of all the powerful biblical arguments against the idea of God using evolution, this book is invaluable.

Professor Andy McIntosh
Leeds

This book is dedicated to my wife, Ruth,
who, for over fifty years,
has been the Lord's promised helpmeet
in my ministry and
who encouraged me to write this book.

'If created things are so utterly lovely,
how gloriously beautiful must be He who made them'
Anthony of Padua (1195–1231).

'On the glorious splendour of your majesty,
and on your wondrous works, I will meditate'
(Ps. 145:5).

Contents

INTRODUCTION 7

1. THE FOUNDATION STONE 10

2. GOD THE CREATOR 15

3. SCRIPTURE, GOD'S REVELATION 43

4. WHAT IS MAN? 56

5. THE FALL: THE FIRST GREAT CATASTROPHE 82

6. GOD'S GRACE: CHRIST THE CREATOR AND SAVIOUR 94

7. THIS WORLD: ITS PURPOSE AND FULFILMENT 104

8. CONCLUSION 116

APPENDIX 1. THE DAYS OF CREATION 119

APPENDIX 2. THE HISTORY OF MANKIND 126

FOR FURTHER READING 139

Acknowledgements

I wish to record my thanks to Mark Roberts (Managing Director, Day One) for his encouragement to write this book and to Suzanne Mitchell for the careful and helpful editing of the manuscript, which has surely improved its readability.

Why another book on this subject? The range of books available through any creation organization or publisher is now huge. Targeted at both adult and youth readers, they cover scientific arguments and the marvels of design in the world and cosmos, educational and environmental issues and much more. The purpose of this book, however, is to look at the theological issues arising from the subject.

Traditionally, the term 'evangelical' has been applied to those who accept the Bible as the authoritative Word of God, which is inerrant, infallible and perspicuous, that is, clear and readily understood (though the meanings of some difficult passages may need expertise in exposition to make them plain). A sound evangelical principle of interpretation of the Old Testament is to determine what the Lord Jesus and His apostles understood by a passage. As we will see in this book, they always understood the Genesis creation account and the chapters following it to be true history.

So, for example, Adam and Eve were real people created by God and from whom the whole human population was derived. Following the creation event, they rebelled against God (usually described as 'The Fall') and were judged for that. Years later, their rejection of God's commands had achieved global proportions so that God judged the whole world in the Noahic flood. In each event we see the ecological effects that arose.

In recent years, however, many evangelicals have abandoned this historical understanding of the record of special creation and reinterpreted it as some form of 'creation by evolution'. Recently, Dr Denis Alexander wrote a book expounding this view.[1] It caused great concern because it was seen to be rewriting Scripture and ignoring the Lord's exposition of the Genesis record. Dr Alexander did accept that Adam and Eve were historical, but he believed that they were early *Homo* species on whom God's Spirit did a spiritual work, so making them in His image.

More recently, in the USA, a movement called BioLogos has gone a step further and is teaching that the biblical record is not historical but rather figurative. Because of the scientific status of some of the Christians involved, even outstanding evangelical theologians have been prepared to abandon the traditional evangelical position on creation.

This book is written to show why the abandonment of the traditional evangelical position of creation is extremely dangerous. As we will see in the following chapters, our fundamental Christian doctrines are founded in the early chapters of Genesis. To reject their historicity undermines our confidence in such essential doctrines as our sinfulness and our need (and God's provision) of salvation. In general, we will not consider scientific arguments, as these are well covered elsewhere.

Aside from the debate about the place of creation in our understanding of biology (including such aspects as 'intelligent design'), one wonders if some of the wider issues affecting our society have arisen because we have abandoned the foundational principles tightly tied to the biblical doctrine of creation. For example, has the loss of the traditional respect for the Lord's Day (by Christians as well as the wider society) been a result of the dismissal of the creation account, thereby undermining the Old and New Testament applications of that divine ordinance? The consequences of this loss of the 'day of rest' are apparent. Similarly, at the present time, there is a wide political move throughout the Western world for a redefinition of marriage and, indeed, a loss of respect for this God-given blessing. Have we, in effect, lost the argument because we have broken the link between the institution of marriage and creation?

A note on terminology: when people talk about 'creation' in a Christian context, it is thought that everyone knows what is being referred to. Usually it means 'young-earth creationism' and whatever the speaker or writer understands by that term. The term 'creation' has traditionally been understood to refer to the account given in the early chapters of Genesis. But, like so many other words, it has been hijacked and it is often unclear precisely what is meant.

There is a range of definitions of 'creation' that might be used to describe our understanding of the Genesis account. 'Biblical creation' is a good one and immediately locks the discussion into the Bible account. It is a term that I have used very happily. However, some evangelicals who believe in evolution would protest that they, too, believe in biblical creation, even though they can do so only by reinterpreting the clear sense of the biblical account.

For the purposes of this study I am therefore using the term 'special creation', as this is a little more focused, picking up the biblical message that each aspect of life (and, indeed, of the non-living world) was a special and specific creation by the LORD God. Beyond that, I am not proposing any specific 'creation model', as this would divert from the main issue of the book.

Also, to avoid any misunderstanding by non-Christians, I refer to the God of the Bible, the One and Only true God, known by His personal name YHWH (Jehovah in older English texts).

J. H. John Peet

Note

1 **Denis Alexander,** *Creation or Evolution: Do We Have to Choose?* (Oxford: Monarch, 2008).

The foundation stone

I do not remember much of what I was taught in my English literature lessons at school, but one thought has always stuck in my mind: notice carefully how the author begins his presentation. That is a good principle to follow when approaching the Bible, too. When we consider how many different 'books' there are in the Bible, and how many different authors there were, we realize that we are faced with a remarkable document. Of course, we know that this is ultimately due to the Holy Spirit, the One who moved the men in their writings so that they accurately communicated what the Lord God wanted to be said and kept it free from error.

The Bible's opening ten (in the English text) words are, I believe, the most important ever written, because of their implication:

In the beginning, God created the heavens and the earth.   (Gen. 1:1)

בְּרֵאשִׁית בָּרָא אֱלֹהִים אֵת הַשָּׁמַיִם וְאֵת הָאָרֶץ:

When we turn to the early chapters of Genesis, we must ask what they are saying from God's viewpoint. Too many people, from laypeople to scholars, can only read these chapters in a non-biblical light. There is a danger that Christians can fall into this trap too, even to the extent of treating them in a different way from the rest of the Bible. This has wider implications for scriptural understanding, as has been demonstrated in the last couple of centuries. Once these chapters can be selectively dismissed as unhistorical, the same approach can be used in dealing with anything miraculous in the rest of the Bible, or those historical events that cannot yet be corroborated archaeologically (or, indeed, when considering something that is inconvenient in today's 'politically correct' society). Yet Kline makes the point well: 'Literary analysis of Gen. 1–11 points to the same conclusion. These chapters cannot be identified as non-historical on the basis of any generally applicable literary criteria. Neither are they distinguishable from Gen. 12–50 by significant differences in their literary character.'[1]

The remarkable thing about the early chapters of Genesis that cover the creation, the fall of man, the flood of Noah's day and the dispersion of man at Babel is how they are a kingpin that binds so much of the rest of Scripture together. Genesis 1–11 *is* a foundational statement. Table 1 gives a quick and selective summary of how these chapters are reflected across the Bible. It is not complete, and may not be the best summary, but it does give a perspective to this theme.

Genesis	God's testimony
Exodus	creation in the commandments
1 Chronicles	genealogy of kings of Judah back to Adam
Job	God's own sermon on creation and its implications
Psalms	worship of God as Creator
Isaiah	the uniqueness of the Creator, in contrast to the gods made by man
Gospels	Christ's applications of the Genesis account
Acts	the unity of man and relevance to the gospel
Writings of Paul	creation fundamental to the resurrection, the supremacy of Christ, etc.
Hebrews	acknowledgement of God as Creator signifies our faith in God
Peter	the early chapters of Genesis speak of God's patience and judgement
Jude	uses Adam, Cain and Enoch to demonstrate God's grace and judgement
Revelation	God is worshipped as Creator and described as the Creator of the new heaven and earth

Table 1: The early chapters across the Bible

We naturally think of Genesis as our source of information on creation, but it is interesting to see how much more is said on creation throughout Scripture, developing the Genesis account. For example, creation is mentioned even more frequently in Isaiah's prophecy than in Genesis. One significant passage is the following:

For thus says the LORD,
who created the heavens
   (he is God!),
who formed the earth and made it
   (he established it;
he did not create it empty,
   he formed it to be inhabited!):
'I am the LORD, and there is no other.'   (Isa. 45:18)

Taking a passage like Isaiah's, where he contrasts the Creator to the gods of the heathen, one wonders whether theistic evolutionists have 'created' a God based on their own ideas rather than accept who He claims to be. It seems that they wish to redefine Him and His works in contradiction of what Scripture says.

When Job was oppressed by his troubles and demanded that God give account of Himself for His dealings with him, the LORD responded with a creation sermon. How do theistic evolutionists interpret God's plain claims there to have made each creature specifically for its role in the created order? If God didn't really do that, aside from the fact that it makes Him to be a liar, Job was left with a non-answer as the LORD's argument has lost its force.

Those opening words of the Bible are, then, a foundation on which the rest of Scripture is built; as the psalmist says, 'If the foundations are destroyed, what can the righteous do?' (Ps. 11:3). They are foundational in that, for example, they are concerned with the 'first' events relating to the characteristics of our world: the first man and woman, the first marriage, the first sin, the first judgement, the first murder, the first covenant and so on.

But, as we look more closely into the Scriptures, we will see how far reaching this foundation is. It affects not just the creation record itself, but also our body of doctrine, our morality, our social behaviour and even our approach to the sciences—and more. It is my purpose to look at the doctrinal implications; then we will see how those, in turn, affect the other issues. We cannot compartmentalize 'origins' as a mere technical issue: it is absolutely foundational. Leahy sums up the issue: 'If the first eleven chapters of Genesis are rejected, then the whole Bible is undermined and the idea of redemptive history is rendered meaningless.'[2]

When we consider how our doctrinal basis rests in these early chapters of Genesis, we realize that, if the record is merely unreliable poetry, as many would suggest, there is a fundamental contradiction between these chapters and the rest of Scripture. For example, if God is not wholly reliable in His statements here, how can we trust Him elsewhere in the Scriptures? And, indeed, our doctrine of God at this point is flawed.

The range of doctrines we will consider includes the following:

God
Scripture
Christ
Man
The Fall
Salvation
Eschatology
Nature

Table 2: Some of the biblical doctrines tied to the Genesis record

Chapter 1

Notes

1 In **D. Guthrie** and **J. A. Motyer** (eds.), *New Bible Commentary* (Leicester: IVP, 1970), p. 80.

2 **Fredrick S. Leahy,** *The Hand of God* (Edinburgh: Banner of Truth, 2006), p. 200.

God the Creator

A non-evangelical writer, the late Langdon Gilkey, once commented, 'Among all the activities of God, creation is that activity which sets Him apart as God.'[1] If Mr Gilkey was right on this point (and would any dispute it?), what does the theistic evolutionary interpretation of the early chapters of Genesis tell us about God? Paul makes the same point: 'For his invisible attributes, namely, his eternal power and divine nature, have been clearly perceived, ever since the creation of the world in the things that have been made' (Rom. 1:20). So what does theistic evolution tell us about God?

We often say that Genesis 1–2 is about creation. That, of course, is true, *but* this passage is even more fundamentally about God in His attributes and actions. Around thirty times in Genesis 1 we read about God. 'God created … moved … said … divided … called … made … set … saw … blessed …' Any discussion of the doctrine of God must start here. Any denial of the truth of the statements written here must undermine the subsequent truths revealed about our amazing God.

It is indisputably true to say that the Bible presents our LORD God as the intelligent cause of creation. To dismiss Him as the cause is unscientific, as it is a basic tenet of science that every effect must have a cause. To resort to the idea of 'nothing' turning into everything without a cause (as the Big Bang theory does) is unscientific.

We are continually being presented with weird and wonderful ideas to explain the universe. Those who present these complex theories, however, are also continually looking for evidence to justify their claims and seeking further ways to explain them. Yet they abandon God because they cannot explain Him.

The Genesis account uses three verbs to describe God's creative work:

bara ('create'), *asah* ('make') and *yatsar* ('form'). They carry the same thought but have their own specific emphases. It is interesting to see them in context. For example, referring to man's creation: 'Then God said, "Let us *make* man in our image ..." So God *created* man in his own image ... then the LORD God *formed* the man of dust from the ground ...' (Gen. 1:26–27; 2:7).

The three verbs are used in Isaiah to describe God's purpose in the creation:

For thus says the LORD,
who *created* the heavens
   (he is God!),
who *formed* the earth and *made* it
   (he established it;
he did not *create* it empty,
   he *formed* it to be inhabited!):
'I am the LORD, and there is no other.'   (Isa. 45:18)

When referring to the creation of man, Isaiah uses these words again (like the Genesis account): '... everyone who is called by my name, whom I *created* for my glory, whom I *formed* and *made*' (Isa. 43:7).

Bara is not used uniquely concerning a creation *ex nihilo* (it is used for providential acts too), but it is used only of the divine acts and not of human efforts. Berkhof notes that *bara* 'serves to stress the greatness of the work of God'.[2]

God is sovereign

Genesis 1:1 speaks of action by the supreme Sovereign who is all-powerful. If this verse is not for real, when and where is reality to be found?

Each action mentioned in Genesis 1 is the giving of a command; it is specific and deliberate, directed to a specified outcome. 'And it was so' (1:7, 9, 11, 15, 24, 30).

What a contrast to the evolutionary approach! Does life arise by God's sovereignty or by purposeless, undirected chance? But chance does not cause anything to happen; it is impotent. The conflict between these two approaches is apparent. Evolution dethrones God by declaring Him to be unnecessary.

Consequently, throughout Scripture, creation and God's sovereignty are tied together. For example, when Peter and John were arrested for their testimony to the Lordship of Christ, the church gathered in prayer. What was the basis for their appeal? 'Sovereign Lord, who made the heaven and the earth and the sea and everything in them ... look upon their threats ...' (Acts 4:24, 29).

Nature has no ability of its own to determine its outcome. It is a Godless system, in spite of the attempts to refer to it as 'Mother Nature', 'Gaia' and so on. God is separate from it and sovereign over it. Surely this is the clear teaching of the whole of Scripture? 'For you, O LORD, are most high over all the earth; you are exalted far above all gods' (Ps. 97:9).

Strangely, one reads of evangelicals who acknowledge that God controls the destiny of nations and mankind but hesitate to grant Him that authority over nature. Yet according to Scripture, He rules over it and clearly controls it. Nature has no will of its own; it does what He commands. This is demonstrated again in Genesis 3, with the judgement, and in the later biblical miracles (of which creation itself is an example).

If God's sovereignty does not extend to nature, what hope is there for us regarding other aspects of His sovereignty? For example, can we have confidence in the proverb 'The heart of man plans his way, but the LORD establishes his steps' (Prov. 16:9)?

God is powerful

This truth obviously goes together with God's sovereignty but it needs to be stated specifically. In contrast to man, who can have good intentions but lacks the ability to fulfil them, God is able. We have already noted that in Genesis 1, when God spoke, it was done. He is omnipotent, all-powerful.

Matthew Henry grasps the wonder of this in his comment on Job 26:7: 'The vast terraqueous globe neither rests upon any pillars nor hangs upon any axle-tree, and yet, by the almighty power of God, is firmly fixed in its place, poised with its own weight. The art of man could not hang a feather upon nothing, yet the divine wisdom hangs the whole earth so.'[3]

He is able to do it. One of the hazards of arguing in defence of Scripture (which does not need our defence!) is that we can be tempted to 'explain away' the miraculous record of Genesis 1 in terms of scientific theory. That is wrong. Creation is not the result of normal scientific processes but of miracle, by the Word of God. Miracles cannot be explained except as the actions of Almighty God. They are normal to Him.

Often we find that Christians who try to explain the creation account scientifically end up trying to explain away other miracles. There is no need to do that here or elsewhere. God is able.

It is interesting to notice that the New Testament confirms God's ability to create from nothing and even makes it a principle of faith in Him (Heb. 11:3). All things which exist were called into existence by this powerful word of God: 'God ... calls into existence the things that do not exist' (Rom. 4:17). The psalmist tells of His powerful voice: 'The voice of the LORD is powerful; the voice of the LORD is full of majesty' (Ps. 29:4). We are told in Genesis 1 that it was by this voice that He created all things.

This truth is repeated elsewhere, such as in Psalm 33:6. That verse goes on to warn us of the implications of seeking to deny such a fact (vv. 8–9). To declare that everything has come about by evolutionary chance processes is to rob Him of His majesty. Dare we do so?

We will return to this again in Chapter 6, but it is worth considering the miracles of Christ at this point. These actions were those of the Creator God (John 1:3). He turned the water into wine (John 2:9), again by His word (vv. 7–8). He did not make the water simply look like wine or taste like wine, but it actually became wine, with all the complexities of wine. Notice too that it was 'the good wine' (v. 10). Could the Creator have done anything less? He also multiplied the loaves and fishes; He calmed the stormy waters; He healed the sick; He raised the dead to life.

The same power raised Christ from the dead and cleanses the sinner from his or her sin. Isn't that harder than the creation of the heavens and the earth from nothing? If the non-Christian can believe that everything came from nothing by an undirected Big Bang, why do some Christians doubt that our all-powerful God could create *ex nihilo*?

There are significant parallels between the openings of the Old and New Testaments. Both are concerned with the miraculous. The forming and filling of the universe was a miraculous act accomplished by the power of God, just as the forming of the Babe in the womb of Mary was miraculous and accomplished by the power of God (Luke 1:35). Moreover, both events involved the overshadowing of the Holy Spirit (Gen. 1:2). Both events are treated with scepticism by the unbeliever as both are 'unscientific'; here is the same process, the same power and the same Holy Spirit.

One fascinating scientific idea of recent decades is Complexity Theory. This indicates that natural systems are controlled by so many variables that it is impossible to produce one equation that will satisfactorily predict an outcome. The classic example is the weather, which is so sensitive to various effects that it is described in terms of the 'butterfly effect' in which a butterfly flapping its wings in one part of the world can upset the equations for the entire planet! The Lord Jesus alluded to this in His reference to the wind (John 3:8). Yet in contrast to our inability, God is so great and powerful that He knows it all and prophesies accurately.

This truth is important to *our confidence in God*. For example, the psalmist spoke of God's ability to create by His powerful word: 'By the word of the LORD the heavens were made ... For he spoke, and it came to be; he commanded, and it stood firm' (Ps. 33:6, 9). He then went on to say that, as a result of this, he could have confidence as he faced his enemies: 'The LORD brings the counsel of the nations to nothing; he frustrates the plans of the peoples ...' (v. 10; see also vv. 11–17).

The prophet Isaiah also referred to God's strength as Creator and named this as *a source of our strength* (Isa. 40:27–31) and therefore confidence. Habakkuk (ch. 3) based his faith in God's punitive actions against Israel on His work in creation and history. As we have already noted, the early church also drew their confidence during persecution from God's creative acts: 'Sovereign Lord, who made the heaven and the earth ...' (Acts 4:24). This prayer would have lost its strength if 'made' meant something more akin to a theistic evolutionary process.

The psalmist speaks of God's powerful word and calls us *to worship the LORD* because of it: 'Let them praise the name of the LORD! For he commanded and they were created' (Ps. 148:5). Or is our worship misplaced because He did not so command?

Paul links God's powerful word to our salvation: 'God, who said, "Let light shine out of darkness," has shone in our hearts to give the light of the knowledge of the glory of God in the face of Jesus Christ' (2 Cor. 4:6). Genesis 1 says that this command was immediately fulfilled ('It was so'); there was never any failure (contrast evolution). A sudden creation therefore implies that He is able suddenly to save. If He didn't do the former, can I be confident in the latter?

That word by which He creates is our source of life, according to Moses: '... that he might make you know that man does not live by bread alone, but man lives by every word that comes from the mouth of the LORD' (Deut. 8:3). These words were quoted by our Lord when dealing with the temptation (Matt. 4:4; Luke 4:4). Again, we see a thread from the creation account through to fundamental New Testament teaching.

Some years ago, a writer in *The Times* newspaper made a valid point: 'If they [theologians who dismiss 'creation' as historical and miraculous] regard Genesis as mythical because it is contrary to science, why is that not also a good reason for rejecting the resurrection—which stands, to say the least, scientifically improbable?'[4] As Phillip Johnson has also pointed out, if we repudiate God's power and authority in creation, we repudiate His laws and morals, for we are told that 'God said' in each.[5]

God is good

But the Genesis record takes us to a further important point. God is sovereign and able, *and* He is good. His creation reflected His character such that He whose standards are high, true and absolute could say repeatedly, 'It is good' (Gen. 1:10, 12, 18, 21, 25). When the whole work was done, He declared, 'It is very good' (1:31). Surely this suggests that God looks down on His work with great contentment. Likewise, the people testified of our Lord Jesus, 'He has done all things well' (Mark 7:37).

To dismiss God's goodness in Genesis 1 (either by implication or direct statement) is to question it elsewhere. We all believe we know what is meant by 'good', yet some would dispute it here. Contrast God's view of the creation as 'good' with the process of evolution, which involves disaster, death, extinction, earthquakes, asteroid impacts and so on. The evolutionary process can hardly be described as 'good'. It is based on undirected mutation, aggression and death: the very things that, according to Scripture, are the result of God's *curse*. If God cursed creation from its inception, there is no answer to evil, pain and death. Death is defined in Scripture as the 'last enemy' (1 Cor. 15:26).

The meaning of the word 'good' in Scripture is 'beautiful', 'fit for purpose'. A glance at any dictionary of biblical words will underline the breadth of meaning of this word: fine, right, pleasing, beautiful, favourable, precious, satisfying, attractive, healthy, pleasant—to quote a few alternative renderings. This concept of goodness (and 'very good' at the end of the six days) is underlined in Genesis 2:18: man's loneliness was not good and he needed a partner to perfect the work. In Jeremiah 8:15, goodness is linked to peace. Yet one of the problems in trying to relate the stages of creation in Genesis 1 to the geological column and its fossils is that one is about 'good' and the other is about destruction.

The goodness of God is demonstrated throughout the Bible and throughout the creation by reference to beauty. Concerning the stars, we are reminded that even though they are innumerable (Gen. 15:5), He knows their number (Ps. 147:4); they are also variable in colour (1 Cor. 15:41), they are all named by God (Isa. 40:26) and they are all controlled by Him (Job 38:31–32). If He so cares for the stars, how much more does He care for us!

We began by pointing out that the early chapters of the Bible are foundational. This is clearly true when it comes to this topic of the goodness of God, which is a fundamental truth about God. For example, when He revealed Himself to Moses, the LORD said, 'I will make all my goodness pass before you and will proclaim before you my name "The LORD". And I will be gracious to whom I will be gracious, and will show mercy on whom I will show mercy' (Exod. 33:19). David declared, 'Oh, how abundant is your goodness …!' (Ps. 31:19). Another psalmist also responded with praise to God's goodness in creation: 'May the glory of the LORD endure for ever; may the LORD rejoice in his works' (Ps. 104:31). If Genesis 1 defines goodness and has to be interpreted by evolutionary processes, what must we deduce about the goodness of God elsewhere?

God must create that which is consistent with His character. Was He powerless to prevent pain? Did He enjoy seeing His creatures suffer? If that were so, it would make Him no different from the gods of the heathens.

But we can be more specific in our understanding of God's goodness in His creation. This is important in the light of His claim in Exodus 33:19, quoted above. God is good to man. The clear suggestion of the creation account is that God created the *home fit for man*. It was only when the rest of the creation was complete and fit for man that God created Adam and Eve. There is a significant parallel to this in what Christ is doing now: He is preparing a *home fit for us* and, when it is ready, He will come again and take us to that home (John 14:2–3).

Furthermore, God created the Sabbath for man. The existence of the week and the day of rest is no accident or coincidence. What is the origin of the week? The day is defined by the rotation of the earth on its axis; the month is defined by the cycle of the moon around our planet; the year is the period of time taken by the earth on its motion around the sun; but there is no scientific definition of a week. Yet it is clearly fundamental to our needs as humans and its existence can be traced back to our early history. In fact, through the Bible we can trace it back to man's creation. Our Lord Jesus made this plain: 'The Sabbath was made for man, not man for the Sabbath' (Mark 2:27). Attempts through history to redefine the week have failed. It is clearly a part of God's plan and not an evolutionary accident.

How good is our God!

God is wise and omniscient

King Solomon wrote,

The LORD by wisdom founded the earth;
    by understanding he established the heavens;
by his knowledge the deeps broke open
    and the clouds drop down the dew.   (Prov. 3:19–20)

Again we see God's wisdom and knowledge plainly in the creation account. God knew what He was doing and worked deliberately. Each plant and animal was created to fit into a specific environment. For example, God said, 'Let the earth sprout vegetation, plants yielding seed, and fruit trees bearing fruit in which is their seed, each according to its kind, on the earth' (Gen. 1:11). We see no struggle here for a fish to survive on land or a reptile to fly in the air (1:20–21).

It is interesting that even Richard Dawkins acknowledges the implication of design. In his book *The Blind Watchmaker*, he says, 'Biology is the study of complicated things that give the appearance of having been designed for a purpose.'[6] In *River out of Eden* he adds, 'The illusion of purpose is so powerful that biologists themselves use the assumption of good design as a working tool.'[7] Of course, he dismisses design as apparent. In contrast, an increasing number of scientists (of varying backgrounds) are recognizing that their scientific studies suggest intelligent design. Only 'special revelation'—God's own statements in Scripture—indicate who that Designer is.

From the creation account we conclude that God's design was perfect. That, of course, is all that we would expect from His nature. But we can go further and note that He is the wise and omniscient Creator. He knew, for example, the requirements of a perfect design. Often it is argued that His work was not perfect as it is considered to be less than ideal. Yet to even argue that way is to display *our* ignorance. A perfect design is one that is optimal: that is, it is perfectly fit for the real world; and the LORD knew what that is. It is no use designing a car that can only be safely driven in a flat, smooth area the size of a continent and with no obstacles (cars, pedestrians, cyclists, road junctions, etc.). It must be fit for real roads in real towns. So it was with the creation of the living world.

As modern scientific research uncovers more in the field of genetics, it is apparent that God built into the genome sufficient variability to allow living organisms to adapt to changing environmental conditions. That was the work of an all-wise God who knew our future needs. Other aspects of the genome also speak of amazing design, but that discussion is beyond this book's brief. Opponents of special creation point to mutations, but that topic will be considered under the doctrine of the Fall in Chapter 5.

God's design was realistic and not a trial-and-error approach in which He 'hoped for the best'. Creationists find it strange when fellow-believers reject the principle of intelligent design. Do such Christians really believe that God was not, and is not, involved? The creationist approach is a recognition of the purposeful, wise Designer and so we look for evidence of that in the world around us—and we find an abundance of such evidence.

God is in control

The creation account ends with the seventh day: 'And on the seventh day God finished his work that he had done, and he rested on the seventh day from all his work that he had done. So God blessed the seventh day and made it holy, because on it God rested from all his work that he had done in creation' (Gen. 2:2–3). This is reiterated in the fourth commandment in Exodus 20:11. The passage does not say that God rested because He was tired, but that He rested from the work of creation. We are reminded in Isaiah 40:28 that 'He does not faint or grow weary'.

These verses in Genesis are often misread and misquoted to imply a deistic approach, that is, that God had stopped working and 'sat back' to let the universe run itself. That is not what the Scriptures say. He rested from creating. It would not make scriptural sense if He stopped His involvement. The universe depends on His continuing work. He now sustains it.

This is summed up by the writer of the Hebrews: 'he upholds the universe by *the word of his power* [or 'his powerful word']' (Heb. 1:3, emphasis added). This is the same word and the same power that created the universe. God is involved intimately in all of our world. That's why the miracles are natural to Him. The word 'upholds' is one frequently used to describe how He keeps and preserves His people.

Scientists talk about the 'laws of nature' and confess that they are essential to their interpretation of the universe. It is a term which explains the regular, repeatable events of the created world. It gives scientific research its predictability. But not only was it God who established these laws (e.g. Job 38:33), but also they reflect His character (Rom. 1:20): He expresses Himself in them. Vern Poythress makes the point that God's character is demonstrated in these laws just as it is in creation as a whole and man in particular.[8] For example, we think of God as *omnipresent* and as *eternal*. The scientific laws reflect this in that they are applicable in any way and at all times (though they are obviously not eternal). Just as the Lord is declared to be the same yesterday, today and for ever, so the scientist can use these laws to explain past, present or future processes. Poythress continues to relate them to our God's nature by showing them to be both knowable and incomprehensible, good, beautiful and so on.

If these laws did not exist, the regularities of scientific explanations would not be possible. More than that, if and when scientists ever reach the ultimate position of being able to explain everything, they still will not have explained these laws of nature on which everything depends.

The Scriptures tell us of God's continuing control of the universe. We live in an orderly world. God made the non-living world to order (Prov. 8:22–31). He made the animals fit for their natural homes (Prov. 30:24–28). He established the laws of the cosmos (Job 38:33; Ps. 136:5–9). If Genesis 1–2 is wrong, these references are also wrong and the writers are unreliable.

The German theologian Helmut Thielicke made a very relevant point in a sermon when referring to God's promise after the Flood: 'Summer and winter, day and night, seedtime and harvest—these are not to be understood as manifestations of natural law at all, but rather as signs that point to the Lord, who is at work here.'[9] What, though, if these natural laws are just incidental results of the Big Bang?

Also implied in these facts is another: God is a worker. This means that work is good. Indeed, Genesis tells us that man is appointed to be like God as a worker (1:26; 2:15). Just as God enjoyed and enjoys His work, so it is His intention that we should do the same. Obviously, like everything else, the nature of our work has been spoilt by sin (see Ch. 5). In the 'new heaven and new earth' we will be workers again, but as God intended it to be.

God is love

We shall see more of this attribute when we consider Genesis 3 in Chapter 5. In fact, His love is tied to His holiness. Perhaps it is because these early chapters are dismissed that so often God's holiness and love become disconnected in man's thinking and His holiness and justice seem to be at variance with His love. But it is not so.

We have already seen God's goodness expressed to man in the creation of a home for him and of the Sabbath rest. These are, of course, also expressions of His love to man. But the creation account gives us more evidence of this love in that God provided a wife for Adam. Again, as described above in the section on 'God is good', the woman was beautiful and fit for man: 'Then the LORD God said, "It is not good that the man should be alone; I will make him a helper fit for him"' (Gen. 2:18).

Here we have the institution of marriage. This passage is foundational and defines marriage for all time. The Lord Jesus referred to these verses as the truth about man's relationship with woman:

He answered, 'Have you not read that he who created them from the beginning made them male and female, and said, "Therefore a man shall leave his father and his mother and hold fast to his wife, and the two shall become one flesh"? So they are no longer two but one flesh. What therefore God has joined together, let not man separate.'

(Matt. 19:4–6)

Commenting on Genesis 2:22, Matthew Henry made a powerful analysis of its implication for marriage: 'The woman was made of a rib out of the side of Adam; not made out of his head to rule over him, nor out of his feet to be trampled upon by him, but out of his side to be equal with him, under his arm to be protected, and near his heart to be beloved.'[10] To God, marriage is beautiful. This is a lesson lost in the evolutionary story.

A man is to represent God in his marriage as the one with responsibility and accountability. He shows the character of God in his self-sacrificial love, as Paul writes in Ephesians 5:25. Paul continues in that passage to say that man's responsibility is to beautify his wife (vv. 25–28): it is definitely not to 'put her down'.

To dismiss Genesis 2:18 undermines our Lord's words and the basis for the Christian definition of marriage. Remove these statements and we have the political and social debates of the present day in which the biblical Word has been hijacked.

When man fell into sin, one of the marks was his and his wife's consciousness of their nakedness. Embarrassed by this, they sought to cover themselves with fig leaves (Gen. 3:7). This, of course, was ineffective in the long term. The leaves would die, dry and wither within a day, so the LORD in His love provided them with animal skins (3:21). Even in their rebellion, He showed His love. But He did more than that: He promised the Saviour as the offspring of the woman (3:15). Speaking of God's love, the hymn-writer says,

It is a thing most wonderful,
Almost too wonderful to be,

That God's own Son should come from heaven

And die to save a child like me.   (William W. How, 1872)

This truth about God's love again emphasizes how Genesis 1 must be true; an evolutionary process would not reflect that love in its 'survival of the fittest' scenario. Already, as we touch on the relevance of our salvation to the creation account, we see how closely tied the early chapters of the Bible are to our evangelism.

More about God's love will be apparent in subsequent chapters.

God is holy

A frequent misunderstanding of God's holiness among non-Christians relates to Genesis 3 and is often expressed along these lines: 'God is unfair or petty. All Adam did was to eat an apple [as it is commonly supposed].' Starting from that point, they fail to grasp the message of Scripture on sin. To reject the historical authenticity of that passage similarly undermines the fact of our all being under condemnation because of the sin of Adam, federal head of the human race.

The serpent accused God of lying: 'You will not surely die. For God knows ...' (Gen. 3:4). But God cannot lie (Heb. 6:18). He is the God of truth (see next section below; Rom. 3:4). To say otherwise is to defame God's character. Adam's listening to the devil rather than God was an act of disobedience and rebellion. God's holiness demanded judgement. If we are to understand His love, we must see it against this dark background. This will be discussed further in Chapter 5.

This theme runs through the rest of the early chapters of Genesis (and beyond), with the murders of Genesis 4 and the corruption of Genesis 5. So came the Flood in Noah's day. God's holiness was again displayed in this last event: He must judge sin. Those who dismiss the universality of the Flood have again missed the point. They fall into the same trap of questioning God's Word and misunderstanding His holiness.

In the Flood record there are two statements about Noah that underline the holiness and the love of God: '[Lamech] called his name Noah, saying, "Out of the ground that the LORD has cursed this one shall bring us relief …"' (5:29); 'Noah was a righteous man, blameless in his generation. Noah walked with God' (6:9). These key words contrast with those about Adam, who tried to hide from God because he sinned (3:8).

God is too holy to treat disobedience and corruption lightly. Peter takes up the theme in 2 Peter 3. Those who dismiss the Genesis record of the Flood must inevitably dismiss Peter's argument of the ultimate judgement. We must not confuse God's patience and holiness. Noah was noted as a preacher of righteousness (2 Peter 2:5) and it was the rejection of God's holiness by the rest of the world that led to the Flood. Or was Peter misled? Of course not. The Genesis record is true. If not, according to Peter's argument, the final judgement cannot be global either (2 Peter 3:7).

God's absolute holiness is emphasized by comparing Genesis 3 and the Flood record. In both cases, the judgement was global. Just as we have all come under God's judgement because of Adam's sin, so all the world came under judgement at the Flood, Noah being protected because of his righteousness. We cannot unravel the fundamental links here without questioning God's holiness.

Further, the Law of God is implicit in the creation passages of Genesis. Jewish tradition links the creation account and the Law of God by focusing on the ten times 'God said' in Genesis 1 and the Ten Commandments given at Sinai (Exod. 20:1–17).[11] We can go through the Ten Commandments and see their place in this account:[12]

- *1st commandment:* God's supremacy is clear from the very first verse of the Bible. In contrast to the ancient myths, He alone is the Creator. Creation is not the outcome of a war or love affairs between gods.
- *2nd commandment:* That He cannot be represented by anything

material is apparent from the fact that He is the Creator of things material and is separate from His creation.

- *3rd commandment:* His special name is introduced in the creation account (Gen. 2:4) and His reaction to man's rebellion demonstrates that He cannot be treated lightly.
- *4th commandment:* The specialness of the Sabbath is demonstrated in Genesis 2:1–2.
- *5th commandment:* The special relationship with our parents is made plain first in Genesis 2:24 but continues through the later chapters describing the parent–child relationship.
- *6th commandment:* That murder is abhorrent to God is plain from Genesis 4:8–12 and 9:6.
- *7th commandment:* The sanctity of marriage is upheld in Genesis 2:24 and this is reinforced by the Lord's quotation of this passage in Matthew 19:4–9, where He makes it plain that marriage should be monogamous, lifelong and heterosexual.
- *8th commandment:* Theft is highlighted as contrary to God's law in the events of the Fall (Gen. 2:17; 3:11).
- *9th commandment:* Genesis 3:13–14 clarifies God's thoughts on the matter of truthfulness.
- *10th commandment:* The events of the first murder were centred around covetousness and jealousy (Gen. 4:5–7).

In several of these cases, we see the significance of the Fall itself. It was abhorrent to a holy God.

God is truthful

The fact of God's truthfulness follows, of course, from His holiness and again underlies the creation record. From whence did the record come? Peter tells us that it came from holy men moved by the Spirit (2 Peter 1:21). Paul tells us that all Scripture is God-inspired (2 Tim. 3:16). So when we discuss Genesis, we are not discussing Moses' ideas which had been coloured by his Egyptian learning (Acts 7:22; Heb. 11:26). Nor are they the ideas of learned men from the Babylonian exile which they falsely attributed to Moses. Before we start challenging the Genesis facts, let us be clear whom we are putting on trial.

When we compare the biblical account with the ungodly accounts of the nations, we see a fundamental difference. The biblical accounts of creation, the Fall and the Flood describe God's actions in accordance with His true nature. There is no taint of them having been borrowed from these other sources. Furthermore, when sceptics of the historicity of the Genesis account refer to the Babylonian records, they seem to assume that they were available before the time of Moses (or else the Pentateuch is assigned to the Babylonian exile). Why? There is no unambiguous evidence for that.

When a crime has been committed, the forensic scientists are called in to examine the scene and advise on the likely events from the evidence they have gathered. In a subsequent court case, the prosecution and the defence will call in their own scientific advisers who will variously interpret the evidence. Forensic science is not unambiguous. We see this in our interpretation of the material evidence following the creation, the Fall and the Flood.

In the court case, the key is the witnesses: those who were there and saw and heard the event. If they are shown to be reliable in their testimony, their words, rather than those of the forensics, will determine the outcome. So it is with the Genesis record. God Himself set the standard for two or three witnesses (Deut. 19:15; 2 Cor. 13:1). God is the only Witness to these events and He is reliable. We remember that God is Triune (see below), so we have three Witnesses who agree and cannot lie. No matter how clever our scientists are supposed to be, it was God who was there and gave His testimony to Moses to record.

So, what are the specific issues in the creation account which relate to God's truthfulness? We will consider just two which are often disputed.

One of the challenges is the reference to 'six days' which were followed by a day of rest. At one conference in which I was participating, a student asked why God created in six days rather than in a longer time frame. A colleague responded that the question should really be, 'Why did He take so long?' The Lord Jesus made the answer to this question clear when He emphasized that the seventh day, the Sabbath, was instituted for man's benefit and not the other way around (Mark 2:27).

It is interesting to see how God instituted and named the 'day'. The psalmist seems to have caught the spirit of this: 'This is the day that the LORD has made; let us rejoice and be glad in it' (Ps. 118:24).

Moses, the compiler of the Pentateuch, had no uncertainty about the reality of the six days: 'For ask now of the days that are past, which were before you, since the day that God created man on the earth, and ask from one end of heaven to the other, whether such a great thing as this has ever happened or was ever heard of' (Deut. 4:32). The fourth commandment (Exod. 20:8–11) is another direct statement by God in which He says that He created everything in six days: 'For in six days the LORD made heaven and earth, the sea, and all that is in them, and rested on the seventh day. Therefore the LORD blessed the Sabbath day and made it holy' (v. 11).

So was it 'six days' or were they 'six lies'? This hits at the very heart of our belief in God's integrity. It is more than a question of our simply being mistaken about the meaning of Genesis 1. Why was the nation of Israel to keep the Sabbath? Because God arbitrarily chose one day in seven, or because He knew that this measured the limit of man's working capacity? Here is 'cause and effect'. The Sabbath law was directly based on God's creation activity. The Jews were to work six days and rest on the Sabbath because God used that pattern in His creation work. But note that God is stating that this is what He did. Is His testimony true or untrue? If it is not true, He breaks His own commandment not to lie. Where, then, is His integrity? He has broken His own moral law.

However, if we believe in God's truthfulness, the issue is settled. The 'six-day creation' is non-negotiable.

There is much we can say on this matter and more detail is given in Appendix 1. The grammatical evidence certainly points to six successive normal days (usually described as 'twenty-four-hour days'). We have seen that God is all-powerful and so able to perform miracles. In fact, usually the miracles are instantaneous demonstrations of His power. Here, though, they are demonstrations of His integrity.

In addition, in Hebrews we read of the parallel between the rest after six days of creation and our eternal rest (Heb. 4:3–4). The spiritual rest described in Hebrews 4 is based on the actual rest of Genesis 2:1–3. Hebrews is a book in which the Holy Spirit shows how much better the new covenant is than the old, yet He does not challenge our understanding of the nature of the creation week.

Some incorrectly dismiss this understanding of Genesis 1 as inconsistent with the scientific evidence for an old earth. What has this got to do with Genesis 1? Nothing! Compare the account in Genesis 1 with the rocks and their fossils. They are talking about different events. Creation is about that which is good, beautiful and harmonious. The rocks speak of catastrophe, death and pain. Straight away we recognize that these must be post-Fall.

We can picture this in a timeline:

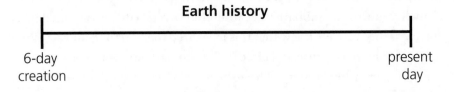

Earth history

6-day creation

present day

All other aspects (including the age of the earth) fall between the two termini. Lest I be misunderstood, let me say that I believe in a 'young earth', again on the basis of the biblical data. On this matter of the age of the earth, it is worth pointing out that the Genesis account is again foundational. Genesis 1:1 opens the biblical record with the statement about God creating the heavens and the earth 'in the beginning'. This is the point at which the clock (time) starts ticking. Another significant reference is the words spoken by our Lord when questioned by the Pharisees about divorce. He pointed them to the Scriptures for the answer and, specifically, to the Genesis account: 'But from the beginning of creation, "God made them male and female"' (Mark 10:6). Note the special creation of humans, and that it was of the man and the woman, and then that it was 'from the beginning of creation'. Not a long time after the creation was begun, but *at the beginning*.

Though no figure is given for the date of the creation week, the genealogies do, of course, provide a timeline. The family tree in Genesis 5 gives a chronology from Adam, via Seth, to Noah and his family. In the previous chapter, we have the line of Cain, and this is clearly consistent with Seth's line in the number of generations. The later chronicler, whose profession required meticulous recording, quoted the succession from Adam without attempting to alter the Genesis detail (1 Chr. 1). He obviously accepted this as a correct record. In Luke's Gospel, this is tied to our Lord's descent (Luke 3:23–38). Jude also accepted these genealogical details (Jude 14). Again, the LORD God seems to be indicating that the Genesis account is a reliable historical record. The genealogies are real, otherwise there is little point to their inclusion. So, we must conclude that the Bible requires a belief in a 'young earth' with an age in thousands of years rather than thousands of millions. If the earth is really very old, surely the LORD would not have deceived us by claiming it was young?

The second matter from the creation account that reflects on our LORD's integrity is found in Genesis 2:2: 'And on the seventh day God finished his work that he had done.' Had He *finished the creation* or not? Did creation continue after that, whether by evolution or otherwise? Let us be clear that by creation we mean the 'special creation' of the 'kinds' of Genesis 1 (vv. 21, 24, 25). No new kinds were to be created as the work was finished. Contrary to frequent accusations, we do not claim that the created kinds were fixed and unable to adapt (often referred to as *microevolution*). We do, however, claim that there were no subsequent new 'kinds'. God had finished His work of creation.

There is a New Testament significance to this. The Hebrew word in Genesis 2:2 is often rendered 'finished' and the Lord Jesus used the same word, 'finished', about the work His Father gave Him to do, namely, our salvation: 'I glorified you on earth, having accomplished the work that you gave Me to do' (John 17:4); 'It is finished' (John 19:30). If we cannot believe Him in Genesis 2:2, how can we believe Him in this matter? If 'finished' does not mean finished, our salvation was not completed at Calvary. Thank God that 'finished' does indeed mean finished in both cases!

It is also of significance that the writer to the Hebrews links the seventh day to our eternal rest (Heb. 4:4), again emphasizing the reality of the seven days of the creation week and the finished work of creation. Hebrews 4:4 could not have been written if Genesis 2:2 were not true. Has God misled the generations until ours?

God is the One and Only

This truth is clearly related to His sovereignty, but it is worth mentioning specifically. I am amazed at how often I hear, or read, evangelical theologians talking about the Genesis account being based on other Semitic stories or written as a reaction to them. There is, of course, no evidence for this in Scripture itself. If the Genesis record is true (as it is), the reverse process is the case, arising from the dispersal at Babel.

Perhaps the one underlying theme that marks out the uniqueness of the Genesis record is the nature of God. The other traditions are generally based on wars between the gods or their sexual exploits. In them, humans are the collateral damage. The Bible account is very different. It is about the loving action of a holy God preparing the earth as the home for man.

The whole account begins with these fundamental words: 'In the beginning, God created the heavens and the earth.' It is the action of YHWH and of Him alone, for there was no other. This verse tells us many things but, above all, that He is the One and Only God. This theme then runs throughout Scripture. As Prof. Bruce Ware expresses it cogently, this verse 'is a straightforward affirmation of monotheism'.[13] This means, of course, that as the sole Creator, He is Lord of all.

Thus there is none greater, none to challenge Him. Paul affirmed the truth of this opening verse in 1 Corinthians 8:6: '… yet for us there is one God, the Father, from whom are all things and for whom we exist, and one Lord, Jesus Christ, through whom are all things and through whom we exist.' How dangerous to dismiss the Genesis account as something less than the whole truth! Where would we draw the line between fact and fiction?

Undoubtedly Moses, as he received this revelation, must have contrasted it with what he had heard from the Egyptians. No doubt the Israelites would also have recognized it as a contrast to the Egyptian ideas they had heard in their captivity. Each day of creation was an attack on the Egyptian gods (see Table 3).

Day	Object 1	Object 2
1	Light (Horus)	Darkness (Set)
2	Sea (Yam)	Sky (Nut)
3	Earth (Geb)	Vegetation (Osiris)
4	Sun (Ra)	Moon (Khonsu) and stars (Hathor)
5	Fish (Rem)	Birds (Nekhbet)
6	Animals (e.g. Apis)	Man (Khnum)

Table 3: YHWH against the gods of Egypt (note that there are alternative gods in some cases and that those named may also have other supposed areas of authority)

The truth of God's uniqueness was underlined by Moses in Deuteronomy 4:19, with a warning of the consequences if this was not observed (v. 24).

God will not share His glory with any other—not even with undirected evolution. God's ultimate glory (Rev. 4:11) is in His creative power. Beware of evolutionists who try to rob Him of His glory.

God is Triune

It has long been recognized that the creation account contains implied references to the Trinity. If these chapters were fiction written by man (for whatever purpose), we would not expect to find evidence of the Trinity, a belief that was not a part of Jewish thinking. The fact that it is here shows that it is divine revelation.

In their confession of faith, called the *Shema*, the Jews quote with conviction, 'The LORD our God, the LORD is one' (Deut. 6:4; see also 4:35). This statement (again given by Moses) is full of significance. In terms of the Trinity, the Hebrew word for God is *Elohim*, which is plural. The word translated 'one' (*ehad*) can also mean 'unity'. Interestingly, this word is used in Genesis 2:24 about the first man and his wife: 'they shall become one flesh'. This leads us to recognize a special truth: that the marriage of believers images the Trinity.

In planning the creation of the man, God said, 'Let us make man in *our* image, after our likeness' (Gen. 1:26, emphasis added); and yet we read 'God created man in *his* own image' (1:27, emphasis added). In these verses 'God' is again in the plural form of the word. So, in the light of further biblical revelation, our confessional statement could read,

YHWH Elohim is but one YHWH,
the Trinity of Father, Son and Holy Spirit.

... unless, of course, this passage is not fact and not true revelation! Yet this Trinitarian aspect of the creation of mankind is so fundamental to Scripture and to the doctrine of man that we *must* dismiss any idea of his evolution from the animals.

The truth of this teaching about the triune God is uncovered directly in the New Testament when we are told that our Lord Jesus, the Word, was the Creator (John 1:1–3). He said, 'I and the Father are one' (John 10:30). This truth is affirmed in 1 Corinthians 8:6, where the Father and Son are each stated to be Creator of all things and of us in particular: '… there is one God, the Father, from whom are all things and for whom we exist, and one Lord, Jesus Christ, through whom are all things and through whom we exist.' Professor Edgar H. Andrews expressed it well when he wrote, '[If] we isolate the different aspects of the work of Christ (in creation, providence, incarnation, teaching, miracle-working, death, resurrection, ascension, redemption, return, judgement, grace and glory), we can become confused.'[14] He rightly points out that it is the whole that is God's master plan.

God the Holy Spirit was active too, specifically moving over the waters (Gen. 1:2; Ps. 104:30; Isa. 40:12–13) and perhaps implied in the breath of God (Gen. 2:7; Ps. 33:6). Elihu acknowledged that we human beings were made by the Spirit of God (Job 33:4). If the creation record is not historical, how does one explain the roles of the Three-in-One? Louis Berkhof makes the point well: 'The work was not divided among the three persons, but the whole work, though from different aspects, is ascribed to each one of the persons. All things are at once *out of* the Father, *through* the Son, and *in* the Holy Spirit [his emphasis].'[15]

This feature of YHWH God is what distinguishes Him from the gods of other religions. Obviously, there are other aspects of Himself and His work that do this too, such as our salvation, but these all reflect on His Triune nature. Here in Genesis 1 we are faced with this fundamental revelation of God and this again reinforces the point that this chapter—

and those that follow it— is a true foundation stone which cannot be dismissed.

God is eternal

Finally, we note that God's eternal nature is declared in the opening verse of the biblical revelation. God created 'in the beginning', so He was already in existence before time began. The Lord Jesus referred to this in John 17:5.

This emphasizes that God is before and over all the creation. He is bigger—much bigger—than it all. If the creation happened by chance, by trial and error, how can we know that He is able to control it? His eternal nature emphasizes that He did not depend on us. Rather, we depend on Him, the One who will bring this created world to an end (2 Peter 3:7) and create the new heavens and earth, by His word. He is eternal and unchanging, and so we can take what we have learned of Him from the Scriptures (even in the work of creation) and apply them to our experience of Him today.

The concept of time, and so of eternity, is one that scientists find challenging. The Bible makes no attempt to explain either of them but it is clear that God is of eternity and man of time. God is Spirit; man is flesh created by God. Unless we accept these biblical concepts as our basic thinking, we are bound to go astray.

This understanding demonstrates, too, the falsity of Satan's tempting words 'you will be like God' (Gen. 3:5). Clearly, as Adam and Eve would have understood it, that was impossible. The characteristics which we have noted in this chapter are not marks of man but of God. This feature in particular—God's eternal nature—is a difference in an immeasurable dimension.

The truth of God's eternal nature is picked up in the New Testament. We are told that before the foundation of the world, that is, in eternity and before time, God planned our redemption: '[God] chose us in him

[Christ] before the foundation of the world' (Eph. 1:4); '... everyone whose name has not been written before the foundation of the world in the book of life of the Lamb who was slain' (Rev. 13:8). Grace itself was given to us through Christ before the creation (2 Tim. 1:9). Eternal life was promised (and so guaranteed) before the creation (Titus 1:2).

What fundamental truths are missed by those who dismiss the historical accuracy of Genesis 1! It was in eternity that the counsels of the Triune God planned everything, including salvation, for you and me.

It is this eternal God who is our refuge (Deut. 33:27) and as the psalmist recognized, 'he who keeps [you] will neither slumber nor sleep' (Ps. 121:4) and will keep us 'from this time forth and for evermore' (Ps. 121:8). Trust Him and His Word; this world will pass away, but our God and His Word are for ever.

Calvin said, 'As soon as we acknowledge God to be the supreme Architect, who has erected the beauteous fabric of the Universe, our minds must necessarily be ravished with wonder at His infinite goodness, wisdom and power.'[16] As I close this chapter, join me in worshipping God our Creator in the words of Timothy Gustafson:

Across the expanse God stretched out His creation—
established the stars, gave the earth its foundation;
His strength claims our worship, His power our fear;
yet Calvary's cross sets us free to draw near.[17]

Evolution impeaches the character of God. Creation glorifies Him.

Notes

1 **Langdon Gilkey,** *Maker of Heaven and Earth* (Lanham, MD: University Press of America, 1985), p. 84.

2 **Louis Berkhof,** *Systematic Theology* (Edinburgh: Banner of Truth, 1958), p. 132.

3 **Matthew Henry,** *Commentary on the Whole Bible*, vol. 3 (Peabody, MA: Hendrickson, 1991), p. 115.

4 **Clifford Longley,** 'Biblical Truths Are of Their Own Particular Kind', in *The Times*, 18 April 1992, p. 12.

5 **Phillip   E.   Johnson,**   'Evolution   and   Christian   Faith',   at http://www.ldolphin.org/ntcreation.html; accessed August 2013.

6 **Richard Dawkins,** *The Blind Watchmaker* (New York: W. W. Norton & Co., 1996), p. 1.

7 **Richard Dawkins,** *River out of Eden* (New York: Basic Books, 1995), p. 98.

8 **Vern Poythress,** *Redeeming Science: A God-Centered Approach* (Wheaton, IL: Crossway, 2006); originally published in *Journal of the Evangelical Theological Society*, 46/1 (2003), 111–123.

9 **Helmut Thielicke,** *The Waiting Father: Sermons on the Parables of Jesus* (London: James Clarke, 1960), p. 87.

10 **Matthew Henry,** *Commentary on the Whole Bible*, vol. 1 (Peabody, MA: Hendrickson, 1994), p. 16.

11 **Karl Löning** and **Erich Zenger,** *To Begin With, God Created* (Collegeville, MN: The Liturgical Press, 2000), p. 113.

12 See, for example, **Carl F. H. Henry,** *Christian Personal Ethics* (Grand Rapids, MI: Eerdmans, 1957), ch. 11; **John Murray,** *Principles of Conduct* (Grand Rapids, MI: Eerdmans, 1957).

13 **Bruce A. Ware,** *Father, Son and Holy Spirit: Relationships, Roles and Relevance* (Wheaton, IL: Crossway, 2005), p. 25.

14 **E. H. Andrews,** 'Christ in Creation', in *Origins* (Biblical Creation Society), 6/15 (1993), 2–5.

15 **Berkhof,** *Systematic Theology*.

16 **John Calvin,** *Commentary on the Book of Psalms*, vol. 1 (Grand Rapids, MI: Eerdmans, 1963), p. 309.

17 **Timothy L. Gustafson,** *Our Daily Bread®,* © 2012 by RBC Ministries, Grand Rapids, MI. Reprinted by permission. All rights reserved.

Scripture, God's revelation

Y ou may think that I ought to have started with this topic, as our attitude to the Scriptures will determine how we react to any doctrinal issue. That is true, but it is also true that our doctrine of God will influence our approach to Scripture, His Word. Since He starts by declaring Himself, 'In the beginning, God ...', it seems appropriate to consider Him first, and it will certainly influence our attitude to these accounts of His creative activity.

So, how do we see Scripture, and in particular its opening chapters? Again, our approach to those chapters will affect our approach to the rest of the Bible.

It is God's Word

The Scriptures themselves make it plain that they are the Word of God. Holy men, said Peter (2 Peter 1:21), were moved by the Holy Spirit to record exactly what God wanted us to know. One thing that must be apparent to any reader of the Bible is that God never modifies His teaching to be culturally acceptable. His words frequently entail a head-on clash with local politics. Indeed, we see this with our Lord Jesus. Even the religious leaders of His day were rebuked for going beyond or against God's Word—which included the Mosaic books and so the creation records.

We need to dismiss one myth straight away. Though it is expressed in various ways, there is a common idea that we should not take the Genesis account literally because God had to address early man in simple picture language as he would not understand ideas such as evolution, which these advocates believe to be fact. But stop! Who said that early man needed simple language? That is an evolutionary assumption, not a biblical one. Adam's mind and thinking had not been damaged by sin at his creation and he was made in the image of God. I believe that he was probably the most intelligent man of all mankind apart from Christ.

Who says that God could not explain evolution in a simple way to a non-scientist? I could, even to a child, and God is the perfect communicator. If God didn't mean the account to be read in the way we understand it, why didn't He say what He meant us to understand? Let's take His Word seriously.

Where is our authority? The traditional evangelical position of authority, 'The Bible says', has been replaced by 'Science says'. Now our interpretation of Scripture has to be subjected to the ideas of scientists. But 'science' is not an independent authority. It is actually only what 'scientists say', the consensus of the current leaders of that community. They are not infallible authorities, so we must not be intimidated by scientific opinion.

If biblical interpretation is subject to scientific opinion, which period of the latter do we follow: 2nd–5th century, 15th–16th century, 17th–18th century, 19th–20th century, or only the 21st century—until the 22nd century arrives?

Are the Scriptures to be subject to fallible human interpretation? The doctrine of 'radical depravity' declares that every part of man has been affected by the Fall—and that includes the mind and our reasoning ability. The Holy Spirit is our interpreter. Job 28:1–11 celebrates man's ability to know things, but verses 12–28 tell of his inability to discern wisdom.

It is trustworthy

The trustworthy nature of Scripture follows from the fact that it is *God's* Word, and we have already noted that He is trustworthy. It is a traditional evangelical understanding of Scripture that it is inerrant and infallible. It is factually correct and utterly reliable. We cannot say that it is wrong in its record of facts or in its teaching.

Some will wish to draw attention to the various forms of writing (prose, poetry, parable, myth, allegory, drama, etc.) and say that we must judge these on their own merits and not assume factual accuracy. There is an element of truth in this; we must indeed identify the genre of the passage and analyse it accordingly. However, there are some things we need to bear in mind. Because a passage is, say, poetic, it does not mean that it is not true. Further, all these different forms of writing have recognizable features in Hebrew, the original language of the Old Testament; yet the early chapters of the Bible do not reflect the non-prose features. In fact, poetic elements within those chapters, such as Adam's song in Genesis 2:23, are noticeable because of their contrast to the surrounding text.

Dr Steven Boyd, professor of Biblical Hebrew, carried out a detailed analysis of the text to determine its literary genre. He considered three possible approaches to the text:

- Is it an extended poetic metaphor which communicates truth, but whose plain sense does not correspond to reality?
- Is it a narrative which purports to be truth but is in fact in error?
- Is it a narrative which accurately portrays reality?

He then studied passages of Scripture which record the same event but in two different genres: poetic versus narrative. From these he was able to identify clear differences between the genres. In the light of this analysis, he turned to the creation account, comparing Genesis 1:1–2:3 with Psalm 104. The result was unambiguous: the Genesis record was indisputably narrative and the psalm was poetic. He concluded, 'The weight of evidence ... is so overwhelming that we must acknowledge that Biblical authors believed that they were recounting real events.' That is, it is a historical narrative.[1]

Though some Hebrew scholars would say that the Genesis author was mistaken in this belief, they acknowledge that he believed it to be fact. The final step is our belief in the inspiration of Scripture. When we read of the life of Christ, His death and His resurrection in the New Testament, we accept it as historically reliable. As we shall see in more detail, the New Testament also quotes from the early chapters of Genesis, treating them as historically reliable. On what basis can we dismiss the latter and still accept the former?

Speaking of the gospel, Paul refers to the creation account thus: 'For God, who said, "Let light shine out of darkness", has shone in our hearts to give the light of the knowledge of the glory of God in the face of Jesus Christ' (2 Cor. 4:6). Clearly, the argument depends on the truth of the Genesis statement. If that statement is not historically correct, the application is faulty.

It is definitive

Most evangelical Christians would say that the Scriptures are definitive in matters of faith, morals, ethics and so on—though even these pillars seem to be crumbling nowadays. Yet the Scriptures are not considered definitive in such matters as creation (Gen. 1–2), the Fall (Gen. 3–4), the global Flood (Gen. 6–9), the Babel dispersion (Gen. 11) nor the genealogies (Gen. 5, 11).

The popular British magazine *Nature* noted that 'Bible study led Newton to scientific discoveries'.[2] One fears that the modern tendency is to reject the Bible. Because he believed God to be a God of order, Newton looked for (and found) mathematical equations to describe the motions of the planets. In contrast, some scientists argue that, because they have found the equations to describe a particular event (and so 'explain' it), they have eliminated the need to believe in God. Genesis 1:1 makes it plain that every aspect of the inanimate and the living worlds, the equations and the laws of nature were put in place by God, not chance.

Of course, as we are reminded by those who oppose us, the Bible is not a scientific textbook and cannot be taken to define scientific theories. The Bible does not, for example, speak of genes or fossils, but we must beware of arguments that conflict with scriptural teaching.

Let us consider an example. If we believe that God created everything 'very good', we also believe He created things with a purpose. A modern example would be the subject of 'junk DNA'. The idea held for a long time was that a huge percentage of our genome was made up of evolutionary rubbish that had no function. On the basis of scriptural principles, creationists argued that this position was wrong and predicted that it would be found that this genetic material has a function. Even as I was writing the later chapters of this book, the scientific community announced that, far from the genome consisting of 98% 'junk DNA', at least 80% of the genome is biochemically functional. They predict that the percentage will increase towards the 100% as research is continued.

Another example of the definitive nature of Scripture and its impact on modern research concerns the historicity of Adam and Eve. The biblical account of their special creation is so specific in both God's words (Gen. 1:26) and His actions (Gen. 1:27; 2:7, 21–22) that there should be little doubt about their true and non-evolutionary origin. Yet we see trends in evangelicalism which should distress us.

Those who espouse evolution have struggled with this truth. Because of their commitment to an evolutionary origin (and its chronological implications), they have been convinced of a link between man and the apes. However, as they will admit, there is a big step between them which cannot be traced unambiguously in the fossil record. Their dilemma comes in handling the Genesis statement that man is in the 'image of God' (see the next chapter). What does this mean? How did it come about?

For several decades, the accepted approach was to see an early form of man, *Homo erectus*, endowed by God with a spiritual dimension which marked him out as different from his contemporaries. He was often nicknamed *Homo divinus*, an 'ape' that bore God's image.

In the last decade, our theistic evolution brethren have gone further and many now reject this idea of a unique couple transformed in this way. They say that Adam and Eve were not a historical couple and that this Genesis account is just a parable to illustrate a spiritual truth. Sadly, a number of evangelical theologians are jumping onto this bandwagon, apparently intimidated by the scientific arguments. This will lead to all sorts of theological problems because of not allowing the Scriptures to define the parameters for understanding the scientific facts.

History tells us that academic studies have frequently thrown up conflicts with Scripture. The sceptics use them as weapons to dismiss the Word of God. Bible scholars become divided over whether to reinterpret the Bible or to challenge the secular studies. Almost without exception the conflict has eventually been resolved—for example, in archaeology, by new findings demonstrating the truth of Scripture.

Obviously, it is right to consider whether we have misread or misunderstood the Scriptures, but we must *not* twist the Scriptures to give ourselves apparent credibility in the academic world. We must develop our arguments with thoroughness to challenge the sceptics. In the present context, creationists need to be biblically thorough and scientifically astute.

The creeping displacement of Scripture to accommodate modern ideas and the abandoning of God's Word has led, and will continue to lead, to a position in which 'anything goes' in our society. An example of how important it is that we recognize that the Scriptures are definitive and that this applies to Genesis 1–2 is marriage. At the time of writing, several countries are trying to redefine marriage. But 'marriage' is not a flexible social or cultural term: it is biblical and arises directly from the creation account. Dr James M. Boice and Philip Graham Ryken quote from the Puritans about the high view of marriage portrayed in Genesis:

… the Puritans viewed marriage as a 'high, holy and blessed order of life, ordained not of man, but of God … wherein one man and one woman are coupled and knit together in one flesh and body in the fear and love of God, by the free, loving, hearty, and good consent of them both, to the intent that they two may dwell together as one flesh and body, of one will and mind, in all honesty, virtue and godliness, and spend their lives in equal partaking of all such things as God shall send them with thanksgiving.'[3]

Does our doctrine guide our research, thinking and teaching? Remember Newton (and others of his time) who let the Bible guide his research and so became a founder of modern science. We should come to our research prayerfully, humbly, biblically and worshipfully. Paul's comment about prophecy is equally applicable here: '… test everything; hold fast what is good' (1 Thes. 5:21).

It is a unity

We have described Genesis 1–11 (the accounts of the creation, the Fall and the Flood, etc.) as a foundation stone to the rest of Scripture. The links between these chapters and the rest of Genesis, as well as the rest of the Bible as a whole, must be beyond dispute and, therefore, show that this foundation stone cannot be dismissed but must be seen as a firm rock on which the whole of Scripture is built.

The argument against these early chapters being true factual history requires an abrupt break with the Abrahamic passages, yet the evidence is not there. They are written as a continuum in history and style. This supposed break requires scholars to demonstrate a change in genre and, perhaps, authorship. Yet this cannot be substantiated.

A similar attack is based on the 'two creation accounts' in Genesis 1–2. But, again, this is the result of a failure to understand the structure of Genesis. A recurring word is *toledoth*, which is variously translated 'These are the generations of …' and 'This is the book of the generations of …' (2:4; 5:1; 6:9; 10:1; 11:10, 27; 25:12, 19; 36:1, 9; 37:2). The *New*

Bible Commentary outlines the structure of the book on this principle.[4] Wiseman sees this as a closing statement to each section,[5] but most commentators favour it as a heading. As the theistic evolutionist Kline puts it, 'Since the genitive in this formula is uniformly subjective, the reference is not to the origin *of the heavens and the earth* but the sequel thereof ...'[6]

Figure 4 illustrates the approach which demonstrates the unity of Genesis and so the historicity of the first chapters. In each case, in moving from one main character to the next (e.g. Noah to Shem), we are looking at the 'line of promise' as indicated in Genesis 3:15. The author, under the Holy Spirit's leading, briefly deals with the lesser characters (those not of the promised line) before moving to the next main character. So, from Noah we get the brief reference to Ham and Japheth and their families before a fuller consideration of Shem and his descendants. After discussing Abram's family, including Ishmael, the focus moves to Isaac. Then the focus moves to Jacob. In Genesis 1 we have God as Creator. The heavens and the earth are covered briefly before turning to look at the main focus, man (Adam), around whom chapter 2 is constructed.

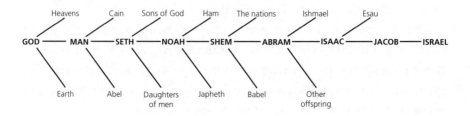

Figure 4: The focus structure of Genesis

We therefore see that the focus in chapters 1 and 2 is different. Chapter 2 is non-chronological and views the world as background to man. This is demonstrated in various ways. The origin of man in the garden is found in both verses 7 and 15, but clearly they refer to one event. Verse 5 notes the absence of plant growth due to a lack of moisture and of man. We are then shown how God provided each. So the creation account is an integral part of the historical structure of the book.

A careful reading of Psalm 104 shows that it is structured around the Genesis account. The psalm is, of course, poetic, but this indicates that the Hebrew writer recognized that the original account is Hebrew historical prose on which his psalm of praise could be based.

It is clear that the Lord Jesus accepted these first two chapters as a unity. In Matthew 19:4–6, when commenting on marriage, He quoted from each chapter—Genesis 1:27 and 2:24—to make His case. He challenged His hearers,

Have you not read that he who created them from the beginning made them male and female, and said, 'Therefore a man shall leave his father and his mother and hold fast to his wife, and the two shall become one flesh'? So they are no longer two but one flesh. What therefore God has joined together, let not man separate.

Christ clearly saw these chapters as complementary and each important to the creation account.

We could go on to show how the Genesis account is foundational to the rest of the Old Testament (see Table 1 for a hint of this), but it is probably more instructive to consider the New Testament use of these early chapters (Table 5). Here we see that every New Testament author refers to some event or events in Genesis 1–11. The gospel references listed show that our Lord referred to each of the first seven chapters. The only chapter not quoted in the New Testament is Genesis 8, but this is an integral part of the story of Noah and so is covered by implication. At no time do these writers (or the words of our Lord Jesus Himself) suggest that the incidents are anything less than historical facts.

NT reference	Subject	Genesis reference
Matthew 19:4–6; Mark 10:6–9	Creation of male & female	1:27; 2:24; 5:1–2
Matthew 23:35; Luke 11:51	Abel	4:4, 8–11
Matthew 24:37–39; Luke 17:26–27	Days of Noah	6:5–6; 7:1
Mark 13:19	God as Creator	1:1; 2:4
Luke 3:34–38	Genealogy of our Lord back to Noah and Adam	5:3–29; 11:10–26
John 1:1–3, 10; Colossians 1:16	Christ as Creator and eternal	1:1; 2:3
John 8:44	Satan the liar	3:4–5
Acts 14:15; 17:24; Colossians 1:16	God created all things	2:1
Acts 17:26	All nations from Adam	9:19; 10:32
Acts 17:28	Man after God's kind	1:26–27
Romans 1:20	Creation	2:4
Romans 4:17; Hebrews 11:3	Creation ex nihilo by His word	1:1–31
Romans 5:12, 14–19; 1 Corinthians 15:21–22	Death through sin	2:17; 3:19
Romans 8:20–22	Creation cursed	3:17–18
Romans 16:20	Satan crushed	3:15
1 Corinthians 6:16	Two become one flesh	2:24
1 Corinthians 11:3–9	Relationship of man to woman	2:18, 22–23; 3:16
1 Corinthians 11:7; Colossians 3:10	Man in the image of God	1:27; 5:1
1 Corinthians 15:38–39	Creation according to kinds	1:11, 21, 24
1 Corinthians 15:45–47	Creation of man from the dust	2:7
2 Corinthians 4:6	Light out of darkness	1:3–5
2 Corinthians 11:3; 1 Timothy 2:14	Serpent deceived Eve	3:1–6

Galatians 4:4	Christ, seed of the woman	3:15
Ephesians 3:9	God created all things	2:3
Ephesians 5:30–31	Man and his wife one flesh	2:24
1 Timothy 2:13–14	Order in creation	2:18–23
1 Timothy 4:4	Creation is good	1:10–31
Hebrews 1:10	God, Creator of heaven & earth	1:1
Hebrews 2:7–8	All in subjection to God	1:26–30; 9:2–3
Hebrews 4:3	Finished creation	2:1
Hebrews 4:4, 10	Seventh-day rest	2:2
Hebrews 11:4	Abel and Cain's sacrifices	4:3–5, 10
Hebrews 11:5	Enoch removed by God	5:21–24
Hebrews 11:7	Noah's family saved	7:1
Hebrews 12:24	Blood of Abel	4:10
James 3:9	Man in the likeness of God	1:26–27; 5:1
1 Peter 3:20; 2 Peter 2:5	Eight saved in the ark	6:14–16; 7:13
2 Peter 3:4–5	Earth formed out of water	1:5–7
2 Peter 3:6	Earth destroyed by water	7:17–24
1 John 3:8	Devil sinning from the beginning	3:14
1 John 3:12	Cain murdered Abel	4:8, 25
Jude 11	Way of Cain	4:8, 16, 25
Jude 14	Enoch, seventh from Adam	5:3–24
Revelation 2:7; 22:2, 14	Tree of life	2:9
Revelation 3:14	Beginning of God's creation	1:1; 2:1–4
Revelation 4:11; 10:6	God the Creator	2:1–3
Revelation 12:9; 20:2	Satan, the serpent and dragon	3:1, 14
Revelation 21:1	First heaven and first earth	1:1; 2:1–4
Revelation 21:4; 22:3	End of the curse	3:17–19

Table 5: New Testament references to Genesis 1–11

Each one of these links listed in Table 5 is worthy of comment, but there is one that is very significant in the context of what we are studying in this book. I refer to 1 Corinthians 11:8: 'For man was not made from woman, but woman from man. Neither was man created for woman, but woman for man.' This statement has no meaning in evolutionary terms as the natural process is the reverse, as Paul implies. It is a point of theological significance and it is only true if Genesis 1–2 is true, for Paul is referring to that creation account (Gen. 2:21–23).

Paul's confidence in the historical truth of the Genesis account is clear when he writes to Timothy, 'For Adam was formed first, then Eve; and Adam was not deceived, but the woman was deceived and became a transgressor' (1 Tim. 2:13–14).

If we doubt Genesis 1, what about John 1? If we question John 1:3, 10 concerning Christ as Creator, how can we trust John 1:12 and 3:16 about Him as Saviour? In John's Gospel, we are presented with the One who is life (14:6) creating life. That is logical. He, the Life-Giver, is the One who gives eternal life (10:10). Similarly, we cannot dismiss Hebrews 1:2 and 11:3 as not factual and still claim the truth of Hebrews 4:15.

Scripture, from Genesis 1 through to Revelation 22, is God's revelation and so is trustworthy and can be taken at face value. To do anything else is to doubt God's Word.

Evolution usurps the authority of Scripture. Creation acknowledges that it is God's revelation and causes us to submit to its authority.

Notes

1 **S. W. Boyd,** 'Statistical Determination of Genre in Biblical Hebrew: Evidence for an Historical Reading of Genesis 1:1–2:3', in **L. Vardiman, A. A. Snelling** and **E. F. Chaffin** (eds.), *Radioisotopes and the Age of the Earth*, vol. 2 (El Cajon, CA: Institute for Creation Research, 2005), pp. 631–734.

2 *Nature*, 430/821 (2004).

3 **J. M. Boice** and **P. G. Ryken,** *The Doctrines of Grace: Rediscovering the Evangelical Gospel* (Wheaton, IL: Crossway, 2002), p. 46.

4   **D. Guthrie** and **J. A. Motyer** (eds.), *New Bible Commentary* (Leicester: IVP, 1970), p. 81.

5   **P. J. Wiseman,** *New Discoveries in Babylonia about Genesis* (London: Marshall, Morgan & Scott, 1936).

6   Ibid. p. 83.

What is man?

This chapter's title is the question asked by the psalmist, but for different and better reasons than we normally have: 'What is man that you are mindful of him, and the son of man that you care for him?' (Ps. 8:4). The psalmist is amazed that God should be interested in us when, set against the greatness of the universe, we are apparently so insignificant. We will be able to answer this question in the context of our subject if we appreciate the psalmist's bewilderment. He is reflecting on the creation account in Genesis, so let us turn back to that passage.

The title of this book refers to 'special creation'. We have seen that this applies to each day in the creation week, but it applies in a very special way to the creation of man. John Murray refers to the difference between the creation of the animals and that of man as '"an abrupt change" that takes place from "after its kind" to "in Our image, after Our likeness"'.[1]

For each part of the material and animal creation, we read that 'God said' and it came about. Concerning man (and his woman), we read that the Trinity had an agreement (Gen. 1:26) and then God made man (1:27). In the second chapter of Genesis we read something more in terms of detail (2:7, 22).

This truth, that God specifically designed and created man, is reiterated throughout Scripture (e.g. Ps. 94:9; 139:14; Isa. 44:24). The last reference is additionally significant because it emphasizes God's special attention not only in the creation of man, but also in that of the cosmos.

Clearly man is special to God, as the psalmist said. The message of creation is that man matters to God. You matter to Him. This is why creation is important evangelistically. Some years ago, I was speaking on creation at a college in Moldova. After the public question time, a young lady came to me, her face glowing with excitement, and said, 'You mean I can know God?' During that week she did indeed come to know Him.

In Psalm 8:4, the psalmist also notes God's care for mankind. The second half of the verse is most significant in that its meaning goes deeper than 'care'. The original wording is 'that you visit him'. This was true in Eden (Gen. 3:8) and on several occasions throughout the Old Testament (usually referring to the 'angel of the LORD', believed to be our Lord Jesus Christ prior to His incarnation). The ultimate act of caring was the incarnation (and subsequent sacrifice) when God truly visited us in the person of the Lord Jesus Christ (Heb. 2:7, 9).

The image of God

As the psalmist continues, he notes something which relates to the creation of man and is the fundamental answer to his question 'What is man?': 'Yet you have made him a little lower than the heavenly beings and crowned him with glory and honour' (8:5).

There is debate concerning to whom the 'heavenly beings' refer, but Genesis 1:27 makes the ultimate nature of man very clear: he is made in the 'image of God'. The word translated as 'angels' or 'heavenly beings' in various translations is *elohim*, which we have seen is also the word for 'God' in Genesis. Along with other commentators, therefore, I believe that this term is directly equivalent to the 'image of God'. In contrast to the secular approach—'Man is a little higher than the animals'—the Bible tells us that 'Man is a little lower than God'. God made man to a model which could not be exceeded: Himself.

Do you notice a precious truth here? We are 'Handmade by God' and 'Designed by God'. Imagine seeing such labels on the goods we buy or are given! But they are on us!

Man is in the *image of God*. 'Image' is used to refer to an impression (Matt. 22:20), not an identical clone. God Himself was the blueprint for the creation of man. We bear God's image, whereas our Lord Jesus, of course, *is* God's image (2 Cor. 4:4; Col. 1:15). There are obvious limitations to this imaging: we are finite; God has incommunicable attributes; man is now imperfect (a distorted image) due to sin. We are not claiming to be the same as God, but to reflect Him, just as the moon reflects the sun. As Paul put it when quoting Aratus, 'For we are indeed his offspring' (Acts 17:28). Literally, we are of 'God's kind'. That reminds us of Genesis 1 again. Each of the plants and animals was made 'according to its kind' (1:11–12, 21, 24–25) and then 'God said, "Let us make man in our image"' (1:26). The point is made again in Genesis 5:1.

Think of the implications: our closest relative is God. With us alone does our God share His communicable attributes (e.g. Rom. 8:29; Col. 3:10), as we shall see below. This is a transforming truth that gives man a unique dignity.

Acts 17 gives us another important theological point: 'Being then God's offspring, we ought not to think that the divine being is like gold or silver or stone, an image formed by the art and imagination of man' (Acts 17:29). Paul argues that, since we are made in God's image, it follows that God cannot be an idol made out of wood, stone or precious materials. One has to wonder, therefore, what would be the significance of this point if we had evolved from ape-like creatures? Contrasting man to the animals, Carl Henry says, 'Man is … superior to all other creatures … by virtue of his ability to know and love his Creator. This … is the *imago Dei*.'[2] Our humanness is the image of God.

The truth of our being made in God's image is reflected by Luke in the genealogy of our Lord Jesus (Luke 3). The expression 'the son of' is simply 'of' in the Greek, so verse 38 literally reads, 'of Enos, of Seth, of Adam, of God'. Not only does Luke indicate the historicity of the Genesis account in terms of the human line, but he also draws attention to the fact that Adam was 'of God'. This underlines other important truths, such as that we are all descendants of Adam and that Christ, too, was, by human birth, a descendant of Adam. Thus, He could represent us all on the cross when He '[took] away the sin of the world' (John 1:29). Our Lord was and is indeed the 'last Adam' (1 Cor. 15:45).

But we need to go further, as does Genesis 1:27 in its emphasis that both the man and the woman were made in God's image. Man was created by the special action of God (2:7); woman too was created uniquely (2:21–22). Theistic evolutionism has no way of interpreting this factual statement.

That man and woman are different is obvious, but separately and together each reflects God Himself. The man was given a position of headship with its responsibility and authority. This is a fundamental aspect of his imaging God (1 Cor. 11:3; Eph. 5:23). The woman was created as the helper (Hebrew *ezer*) for man. This is not an inferior position—it is a term used of God Himself (Ps. 118:7; Heb. 13:6). Together they image God—two persons but one flesh (Gen. 2:24), reminding us of the Trinity (three in one).

We, especially Christians, should demonstrate our relationship with God. We are not (in biblical terms) 'animals' and we should not be 'aping' them. In summary, being in God's image means that, in contrast to the animal kingdom, we are persons.[3] In man, God becomes visible. 'He is the image of God in the fact that he is man.'[4] To be 'in the image of God' is to be 'human'. This image is dynamic, not static; it is active, not passive. We are not museum pieces, but living examples (see Rom. 12:1–2).

So, how is this image to be seen in mankind? Firstly, we need to emphasize that we are created in the image of God. We tend to hear about the use of anthropomorphisms when God is described, that is, God made in the image of man. That is clearly wrong. God is not to be described anthropomorphically; we are to be described theomorphically.[5] As we get it right, we see how different man is from the animals.

The context of man's being made in the image of God is that man was created into a high state into which no other creature was made. It cannot be attained by evolution and was not attained that way. It must, therefore, represent something that is not shared by the animals. That man is different from the animals is apparent from Genesis 2:18–20.

In considering this wonder that God made us in His image, we can go further. Our God is our heavenly Father. This is not an anthropological description of God. Rather, since we are in His image, we must consider the distinctive features of God as Father in order to define the human responsibility of fathers, which the Lord specified as man's role: 'Be fruitful and multiply and fill the earth ...' (Gen. 1:28).

Bruce Ware writes, 'Image-of-God procreation is designed to reveal the pleasure God has in creating people in His own image, and the joy of bringing yet more of these humans into existence. We have the privilege of creating image-of-God persons.'[6] He continues to describe what true fatherhood is, as demonstrated by God, our Father. For example, 'God fathers us by being *lavish, generous, even extravagant in His care, love, provision and protection for His children* [emphasis his].'[7]

Doesn't this give a rich picture of what it means to be in the image of God? Yet this is established in the creation account.

We mentioned in Chapter 2 that Genesis 1 is all about God. So, if we want to see exactly what is meant by being in the image of God, we need to look at God's self-revelation in that passage and in Genesis 2 where it is most fully described. If we dismiss this section of God's Word as a true historical record, we are left with a weak and incomplete—and so deficient—explanation of this aspect of the creation of man, as we find in some of the writings of our theistic evolution brethren.

We also need to realize that man is physical, mental and spiritual. In each of these areas we are imaging God, and in each we are distinct from the apes.

Imaging God in creativity: 'God created ...'
God is the Creator of everything; that is the message of Genesis 1–2 in

particular, though it is declared throughout Scripture. So, if we have been made in His image, we must be creative. That is clearly true, but we emphasize again that there is a qualitative difference: we are finite and so our creativity does not match God's. Also, we recognize that man's creativity can be flawed by sin, whereas God's is perfect. A little thought on this subject emphasizes the gap between man and the animals.

In Genesis 1, when talking of God establishing the 'heavenly bodies', the account tells us that 'God said, "Let there be lights in the expanse of the heavens to separate the day from the night. And let them be for signs … and let them be lights …' (1:14–15). This speaks of deliberate planning. So it is with man.

Like God, we design and construct complex structures. What is very impressive is the *variety* of, say, the buildings we can design. In London, you can find domestic dwellings, cathedrals and huge business structures like 'the Gherkin' and 'the Shard', to give them their popular names. An architect will have a significant portfolio of designs. He or she will select from and use a range of materials reflecting the purpose of the structure.

In the last century or so, we have watched engineers designing a wide range of airborne vehicles, such as balloons, airships, planes (and what a variety of them!) and spaceships. We can also point to clothes designers, interior designers and landscape designers. Even more fundamental are the design, construction and use of tools and machinery for the construction of other things.

Then we can consider artistic creativity. One distinctive feature of design is the incorporation of beauty, which rarely has a functional importance. It is aesthetic. Again, we can apply this to the natural world and recognize the hand of our great Designer. Man's artistic creativity covers art, music, literature and many other areas.

Where do these skills come from? The creation account tells us that it was the outcome of man's special creation. Common sense agrees. Moses says that God had called Bezalel and 'filled him with the Spirit of God, with skill, with intelligence, with knowledge …' (Exod. 35:30–35).

Imaging God in intelligence: 'Let there be …'

The anthropologist and evolutionist Richard Rudgley recognized that man has always been intelligent. He commented in a television programme, 'Stone Age man was as intelligent as we are.'[8]

Again, we note not only the imaging of God but our limitations. The apostle Paul compared the 'foolishness' of God with man's wisdom: 'For the foolishness of God is wiser than men' (1 Cor. 1:25).

With that in mind, however, let us consider man's intellectual ability. We accumulate knowledge. Think of how much a child learns about the world in his or her earliest years, then how he or she moves on through school collecting more information, possibly then going to university with its depth of knowledge and understanding. He or she then continues to accumulate knowledge in adulthood. We are living encyclopaedias of facts and theories.

Another characteristic of humans is their mathematical ability. We can count to unlimited high numbers; we can carry out arithmetic, algebra and geometry. We learn and apply calculus, statistics and mathematical modelling. We can carry out abstract mathematical processes. Dr Marc Hauser has commented, '[As to] what mechanisms evolved in our most immediate ancestors that enabled them to represent and conceptualize numbers … we can only offer a highly speculative answer.'[9] If we remember that our 'ancestor' is God, we can answer that speculation.

We are, indeed, capable of engaging in complex reasoning and abstract thought. Men and women engage in philosophical reflection and in 'lateral thinking'. We develop and test theories; we judge among options; we are, by nature, planners.

Of course, we rarely find someone who excels in many of these aspects, but we are all able to engage in them to varying extents. Our God excels in them all. We are in a different class from the animals—but then we are in God's image, not theirs.

In recent years, we have heard much from and of the 'Intelligent Design Movement'. Its proponents have done valuable work in recognizing not just that there is design in nature, but also that it must be intelligent design. Their weakness is that they have stopped short of facing the question 'Who is the intelligent designer?' The creation message, from the Bible, is that it is God.

The human mind has long puzzled evolutionists. Even Darwin was sceptical as to how it could have evolved from 'the lowest animal'.[10] C. S. Lewis made a similar comment: 'If my own mind is the product of the irrational, how shall I trust my mind when it tells me about evolution?'[11] When we consider the intelligence of man as above, we must agree. Again, we are reminded that the Scriptures indicate that this is another matter in which we image God. Paul writes, 'For who has known the mind of the Lord ...?' (Rom. 11:34).

How foolish are those who, like Prof. Arthur Kornberg of Stanford University, say that 'the mind is only chemistry'.[12] Can we really reproduce mind processes in a test tube? Prof. Noam Chomsky admits, 'The process by which the human mind has achieved its present state of complexity is a complete mystery.'[13] This must be the honest view of anyone who rejects 'special creation'.

In fact, Darwin made a powerful comment:

Another source of conviction in the existence of God connected with the reason and not the feelings, impresses me as having much more weight. This follows from the extreme difficulty or rather impossibility of conceiving ... man with his capability of looking far backwards and far into futurity, as the result of blind chance or necessity. When thus reflecting I feel compelled to look at a first cause having an intelligent mind in some degree analogous to that of man.[14]

Imaging God in communication: 'God said …'

That animals communicate is without question, but the ability and manner of human communication is unparalleled and reflects our divine origin. Indeed, as we go through these aspects of our imaging God, we realize that the gulf between us and the animals in each case is unbridgeable by any naturalistic process.

We have many modes of communication, both verbal and non-verbal. We can convey our messages by speech or song, by laughter or tears, by sighs or shouts, by discussion or debate, by preaching or teaching. In the creation account we read of our God speaking, commanding the formation of the universe and all that is in it. We read of the Trinity communicating among Themselves. Elsewhere, we read of our God laughing. Perhaps one of the most wonderful things is where we read of Him rejoicing over His people with singing: 'The LORD your God … will exult over you with loud singing' (Zeph. 3:17). Picking up from the creation account, John identifies our Lord Jesus as the Creator and the *Word*, so significant is this concept of communication.

Obviously, we can communicate by the written word—but even there we are imaging our God. Concerning the Ten Commandments, we read that the LORD gave to Moses 'the two tablets of the testimony, tablets of stone, written with the finger of God' (Exod. 31:18). In addition, He inspired the biblical writers to record faithfully and accurately His words to us.

We are able to communicate in a variety of languages. Again, this is a God-given ability. Adam on his creation was able to communicate. We read of him naming the animals and his wife—another aspect of our imaging, for God named the day and night, the sky and the seas, and so on. It is recognized by a number of those studying language that language in some form seems to be 'built in' to our brains at birth. At Babel, the LORD caused confusion of language so as to cause the dispersion of the people and thus the formation of the nations (Gen. 11). There is no indication as to whether there was any link between these languages and that of pre-Babel times.

Man is able to invent new languages. One of the best known is Esperanto. Interestingly, rather than succeeding in becoming the single international language spoken by everyone as intended, it has failed. This reminds us of God's intention at Babel (Gen. 11:7).

When discussing in Chapter 3 the debate about the literary form of the Genesis account, we noted that we can communicate by prose or poetry, by parable or allegory, by story or history, and so on. And our God uses them too; He taught us.

Then we can use other means of communication. Many people are noted for their use of hands when talking, but this becomes a powerful tool ('signing') for those who are deaf and dumb. For the blind, we have Braille, a tactile signing. In general, we communicate by various forms of body language: clapping, jumping, eye movement, facial expressions and so on. We are reminded of the benediction, 'The LORD bless you and keep you; the LORD make His face to shine upon you and be gracious to you; the LORD lift up His countenance upon you and give you peace' (Num. 6:24–26).

Imaging God in relationships: 'Let us ...'

Relationships are a key feature in the biblical revelation and are a defining aspect of our salvation (our reconciliation as in Rom. 5:11; 2 Cor. 5:18–19). A few hours before writing this section, in my 'quiet time', I was meditating on God's statement that Abraham was His friend (Isa. 41:8; see also 2 Chr. 20:7). A few days previously, my attention was drawn to the New Testament reference to the same truth (James 2:23). I was struck by the wonder of this possibility. Then I recalled that a similar thing was said of Moses (Exod. 33:11). As I reflected on these amazing claims, I realized that it is true for believers too (John 15:13–15; Ps.

25:14). How important relationships are to God! And how staggering this is for us!

To understand this fully, we need to return to the creation account. In Genesis 1:26, as we have already seen, God said, 'Let us ...', an allusion to the Trinity and Their eternal relationship. As we study the rest of the Scriptures, we can uncover the significance of it. But relationships were what God wanted for mankind too. To the man, God gave the woman (Gen. 2:22–23) as a friend. This is picked up later in the Scriptures to demonstrate the beauty of this special relationship.

Marriage is one of those aspects of human relationships which were instituted by God at creation. It is not a cultural convention and so is not subject to the whims of politicians and society. To redefine marriage to include homosexual relationships is deliberately to set oneself or one's society above God. Nebuchadnezzar set himself above God and was brought down by Him. Without the creation record, however, we have no definition of marriage and man is supposedly free to define it as he wishes. It is significant that those who believe in special creation inevitably oppose the legitimizing of homosexual relationships. Our Lord took up this issue of marriage and noted, from the Genesis account, that it is heterosexual, monogamous and for life (Matt. 19:5).

One of the significant aspects of the Trinity's relationship is in the work They do together. Specifically, of course, Genesis describes Their relationship in the work of creation. We see the Father planning and directing, but we are also given a reference to the Spirit (Gen. 1:2). John's Gospel (as well as Colossians and Hebrews) shows that God the Son was also at work in creation as the Word of God. Likewise, Adam was given responsibility to tend the garden, with Eve being given the responsibility of helping him fulfil this task. So we work together with our marriage partners in our daily tasks and in our spiritual service.

Then, as the psalmist mentions in Psalm 8:4, there is a closeness between man and God. In Genesis 3, we see this declared in a particular way: 'They heard the sound of the LORD God walking in the garden in the cool of the day' (v. 8).

Imagine that experience. It was broken, of course, as a result of man's sin which caused them to be excluded from God's presence (Gen. 3:23–24); in Christ, however, the experience is restored to His people as *we* walk and talk with Him in prayer and in reading the Scriptures.

So, like his Creator, man has a sense of relationship with its love and loyalty. We experience it in our families and also among trusted friends. A significant difference between humans and animals in this regard is its dimension in time and distance. Our friendships stretch across distances and generations. They even reach beyond death. Many of us still feel love and other emotions for loved ones who have died. We remember them and their deeds with affection.

Humans also form relationships in complex and versatile social structures. We do not necessarily consider these to be friendships, but we relate to others who have an impact on some part of our life or work. We learn how to relate to them for our mutual benefit.

One outstanding feature of human relationships is in caring. The psalmist reminds us of this by commenting on how God cares for us (Ps. 8:4). We are, therefore, not surprised to see the extents to which this care can go. The concept of altruism (caring for others without considering the risk or cost to ourselves) has no natural survival advantage and non-creationists have struggled to explain it. Altruism is self-sacrifice as against self-preservation.

This caring attitude results directly from our being in the image of God. In his first letter, John says, '... love is from God' (1 John 4:7): that is why we love one another and God. Another characteristic of man is forgiveness, and this too is a reflection of our God who displayed this forgiveness in the darkest moments (Gen. 3:15; 4:15; 6:18) and ultimately at the cross.

David Templeton wrote, 'It's intriguing to me that when you study nature you learn that nature neither gives nor expects mercy. But human beings really do hold ourselves accountable in a way that other animals don't.'[15] However, since we are made in God's image, we are not surprised to find that the supreme example of this is our Lord Jesus (e.g. Phil. 2:5–8).

Imaging God in morality: 'God saw that it was good'

The words 'God saw that it was good' is more than a statement about beauty—and the creation was certainly beautiful. As we noted in Chapter 2, 'good' means beautiful and fit for the purpose. It is a word used of the creation before it was cursed. God never describes that which is the result of sin as 'good'. Ultimately, then, it is a moral statement. When we look at man, we see how he images God in his sense of morality. Biologist Thomas Huxley is reported to have described this moral difference between man and the apes in terms of man standing on a mountain top, so great is the gap between us.

Of course, like everything else, man's standards and actions have been affected by sin, so his sense of morality is often skewed away from that of the Lord. Nevertheless, we can identify various aspects of it.

Firstly, starting with the immediate Genesis context, man has *an appreciation of what is right* (and, in contrast, what is wrong). These days, we find that attitudes have been warped by the evil one so that what the Bible calls 'wicked' is interpreted in contemporary society as being 'exciting' and 'good'. How often we are seeing God's words twisted and the gospel message thereby undermined.

Though the details of the definitions of good and evil may vary, it is clear that everyone has a general concept of what is right and wrong. Ask a prisoner who has been convicted of heinous crimes and he will tell you what he considers right and wrong. It will also underline how the definitions used by society in general are close to the biblical standards.

One of the things that challenges secular thinkers is how we arrive at our definitions of what is good and what is evil. Prof. Richard Dawkins gives a clear statement of what he considers right and wrong, though he attributes this to evolution. However, he cannot explain how evolution gives this universal standard to which we all seek to adhere. We believe that the standards come from the Bible (e.g. the Ten Commandments—wouldn't it be a wonderful society if everyone kept them?) and are also 'wired' into our consciences.

Secondly, we return to the fact that we have *an appreciation of beauty*. This is something that pervades nature. We look at the flowers and select a beautiful bouquet for our loved ones. We consider animals, perhaps in a safari park, and are stunned by their beauty—some graceful and others bulky, but all provoking comments of wonder. We look at the inanimate world and are moved by its greatness and order. I recall how, as a young man, I stood on the peak of Scafell in Cumbria with a group of fellow Christians and we spontaneously sang, 'How great Thou art!' as we were moved by the panorama before us. The effect of the curse is sometimes apparent, as when we are faced with a deformity. We realize that that is a deviation from the norm and we are reminded of the effect of sin and the consequent judgement.

Because we recognize the difference between right and wrong, and good and evil, we are *able to judge what is worthy of praise or blame*. All the time, often unconsciously, we make such judgements. We readily blame those who spoil or hurt. Hopefully, we just as readily praise that which is good. Again, we see that this is a reflection of our being made in the image of God, who praises the good and judges the bad—and His judgements are, of course, without fault. As we seek to display this feature of His moral character, we should continually check our judgements against His Word and standards.

This leads us onto another aspect of our moral reflection of the image of God. *We have a conscience.* Yes, it is sometimes warped, but the fact that we have one at all is a witness to our creation in the image of God.

Where do we find this sensitivity in the animal kingdom? Paul refers to our conscience in this way: '… the law is written on [our] hearts, while [our] conscience also bears witness' (Rom. 2:15,). He also speaks of those whose consciences have been damaged by sin: '… liars whose consciences are seared' (1 Tim. 4:2). What ape has a conscience and thus a sensitivity to what is right and what is wrong?

Though there are other aspects of our morality, it is worth mentioning just one other by way of illustration: *our recognition of an ethical responsibility*. Whole volumes have been written on this subject, which pervades every aspect of our lives. We are often challenged, rightly, to consider the ethics of what we buy in the shops. Under what conditions do the labourers work? Are they fairly paid? What are we doing to the environment by our pollution or destruction of it in other ways? What about the way employers treat their employees? These and many other ethical issues are again built on Bible teaching, which, in turn, reflects the moral character of God.

Some years ago, I was visiting Russia and was asked to give lectures at a business college on the biblical ethics of economics. The reason for the request was very instructive. Under the communist system, every course included a Marxist ethic which was clearly taught. When the country abandoned Marxism, the college lost an ethical basis for their instruction. They therefore wanted to know the biblical basis underlying our courses. After admitting that in the West we have moved so far away from a Christian foundation to education that we don't have such teaching, I enjoyed opening the Scriptures to them. Even after decades of instruction in atheism and the rejection of Christianity, they knew there must be something the Bible had to say to them.

Imaging God in lordship: 'the Spirit of God was hovering over the face of the waters'

When we study the Scriptures, we cannot help but see that lordship seems to be the primary aspect of man imaging his Maker. We see it in the 'cultural mandate', as it is often called: 'God said to them, "Be fruitful and multiply and fill the earth and subdue it and have dominion over the fish of the sea and over the birds of the heavens and over every living thing that moves on the earth"' (Gen. 1:28); 'The LORD God took the man and put him in the garden of Eden to work it and keep it' (2:15).

Man was given dominion; he did not gain this by his efforts. The relationship with nature was defined by God and was for our benefit and that of nature. Evolutionary theory, however, says that it was gained by means of a battle against the forces around man. As we will see in Chapter 5, this is significant in man's failure to fulfil his commission.

This mandate was repeated after the Flood: 'Be fruitful and multiply and fill the earth. The fear of you and the dread of you shall be upon every beast of the earth and upon every bird of the heavens, upon everything that creeps on the ground and all the fish of the sea. Into your hand they are delivered' (Gen. 9:1–2). It was *the* aspect that the psalmist highlighted:

You have given him dominion over the works of your hands;
    you have put all things under his feet,
all sheep and oxen,
    and also the beasts of the field,
the birds of the heavens, and the fish of the sea,
    whatever passes along the paths of the seas.   (Ps. 8:6–8)

The writer to the Hebrews referred to this as well:

You made him for a little while lower than the angels;
    you have crowned him with glory and honour,
    putting everything in subjection under his feet.   (Heb. 2:7–8)

This management is demonstrated, for example, in the naming of the animals: 'The LORD God ... brought them to the man to see what he would call them. And whatever the man called every living creature, that was its name. The man gave names to all livestock and to the birds of the heavens and to every beast of the field' (Gen. 2:19–20). This was an act of intelligence (discerning something about the creature and assigning an appropriate name) and of authority. To the Hebrew mind, this action of naming something or someone was an indication of the authority a person had. It reflected God's ultimate authority in naming, for example, the heavenly bodies such as the stars.

Lift up your eyes on high and see:
> who created these?
He who brings out their host by number,
> calling them all by name,
by the greatness of his might,
> and because he is strong in power
> not one is missing.

(Isa. 40:26)

The care required in the mandate must, however, carry a responsibility. It is God's creation and He has been pleased to delegate management to us. Adam was the viceroy. The management control is to care for the environment, not to exploit it. Where does this teaching originate if we reject Genesis 1–2 as historical truth? Some have accused evangelicals of encouraging a rape of the environment for our selfish ends. Nothing could be further from the command God has laid on us. Indeed, the wording of the creation account emphasizes this:

When no bush of the field was yet in the land and no small plant of the field had yet sprung up—for the LORD God had not caused it to rain on the land, and there was no man to work the ground, and a mist was going up from the land and was watering the whole face of the ground—then the LORD God formed the man of dust from the ground …'

(Gen. 2:5–7)

The later laws imposed this responsibility on God's people. The animals were not to be ill-treated:

You shall not see your brother's ox or his sheep going astray and ignore them. You shall take them back to your brother. And if he does not live near you and you do not know who he is, you shall bring it home to your house, and it shall stay with you until your brother seeks it. Then you shall restore it to him. And you shall do the same with his donkey or with his garment, or with any lost thing of your brother's, which he loses and you find; you may not ignore it. You shall not see your brother's donkey or his ox fallen down by the way and ignore them. You shall help him to lift them up again.

(Deut. 22:1–4)

The animals too were to share in the Sabbath rest (Exod. 20:9). Even the land we manage for the production of our food is to be given a Sabbath year's rest (Lev. 25:2–7). There are strong warnings against abusing the environment, even in war:

When you besiege a city for a long time, making war against it in order to take it, you shall not destroy its trees by wielding an axe against them. You may eat from them, but you shall not cut them down. Are the trees in the field human, that they should be besieged by you? Only the trees that you know are not trees for food you may destroy and cut down, that you may build siege works against the city that makes war with you, until it falls.

(Deut. 20:19–20)

It is interesting to note that in these passages it is seen that treating the environment correctly works for our benefit.

We are to manage the environment so as to care for the needy, too

(Lev. 19:9–10). We are allowed, for example, to use trees for the construction of homes and for fires, but not to deface them for our own amusement (Ezek. 34:18–19).

The LORD God has provided sufficient resources for all mankind. The fact that some are starving is a criticism of our management and our selfishness.

This lordship over the environment is also something applied to the home (with the man as the head) and in the church (with elders to lead), but in these and other matters we are accountable to God, to whom all these things belong (e.g. Ps. 24:1). If we remove Genesis 1–2, where is the authority and responsibility, and the definition of our lordship?

Imaging God in our spiritual nature: 'the Spirit of God'

We notice too that man, being made in the image of God who is Spirit, has a spiritual nature. Man has the powers of awe and worship. Even the non-Christian displays these characteristics, which mark him out from the animals. Prof. Richard Dawkins, who is an outstanding example of those who oppose God and His work in creation, recognizes this. In an interview in *The Daily Telegraph*, he made the following comment when discussing his love of the tropical rainforests: 'I've contemplated a tropical rainforest and felt a tremendous sense of awe and worship … [pause] … Not, of course, that there is anything to worship.'[16]

However, the true spiritual nature in man has been destroyed by sin and spiritually we are dead (Eph. 2:5). When Adam was created, he was spiritually alive, reflecting his Creator truly in this. But it was, and is, only by the work of God's Spirit that we become spiritually alive. Some say that God took some sub-human creatures and made them spiritually alive. This is not what the Bible teaches. Adam was in communion with God—until he listened to Satan, at which point he died spiritually.

One of the marks of a regenerate person is his or her sense of wonder at our God. When we read of His nature or see His works (not least in our salvation), we break into worship. It is not something worked up but comes from a full heart. The psalmist demonstrates this when he exhorts us to praise the LORD. This is not a law but a delight.

The fact that man has a spiritual nature means that he can be saved and sanctified, each a work of the Spirit of God. The animals cannot experience these things as they do not have a spiritual nature.

Imaging God in our work: 'God finished his work that he had done'

The first verse of the Bible describes God at work ('God created') and the second chapter begins with the statement of Him ceasing that particular work ('God finished his work that he had done'). Exodus 20:9–11 links God's work of creation to our call to work. The work to which man was assigned was defined by God: 'The LORD God took the man and put him in the garden of Eden to work it and keep it' (Gen. 2:15; see also 1:28). So, from the beginning, man was made to image God as a worker.

These references show the good nature of work. God repeatedly described His work as good. Man is appointed to work, imaging his Creator—so, enjoy it! Work was man's purpose in order to give glory to God.

God instructed Adam to rule and fill the earth (Gen. 1:28). This is imaging God's creative work of forming (days 1–3) and filling (days 4–6). The seventh-day rest is, of course, given to us as a further aspect of this relationship with our Creator.

God rested from the work of creation on the seventh day, but not from the work of sustaining the cosmos. In the same way, we rest from our daily labour on the 'day of rest', but, of course, there are those 'background activities' which are a part of our daily lives. It is not a day of inactivity. Rather, it is given to us to make it a day of worship of our Creator God.

The nature of our work has been spoiled as a result of the curse following man's rebellion against God's commands. Work became 'labour', marred by sweat and backaches, by thorns and thistles, by weeds and tares.

> ... cursed is the ground because of you;
>> in pain you shall eat of it all the days of your life;
> thorns and thistles it shall bring forth for you;
>> and you shall eat the plants of the field.
> By the sweat of your face
>> you shall eat bread,
> till you return to the ground,
>> for out of it you were taken;
> for you are dust,
>> and to dust you shall return. (Gen. 3:17–19)

The creation plan was for man to 'subdue' the earth (Gen. 1:28), but, as a result of the curse, the ground now subdues man (Heb. 2:8).

We are not exempted from work because of this. Even our Lord Jesus worked as a carpenter when He became man (Matt. 13:55). It would be good to consider the quality of His work as a model for our attitude to our daily tasks. Indeed, we are to have a sanctified approach to our work, as Paul described it: 'Let the thief no longer steal, but rather let him labour, doing honest work with his own hands, so that he may have something to share with anyone in need' (Eph. 4:28).

Imaging God in our physical nature

Many Christians are uncomfortable with this claim of our imaging God physically since He does not have a body. That is correct, but it is not the claim we are making, as we shall see. God spoke of making man 'in our image'. Man, as we said previously, is physical, mental and spiritual, but in every aspect we are imaging God.

Prof. John Murray made the point that it is not just in his spirit that man is made in God's image:

It would be easy to say [that it is only in his spirit]. God has no body. But it is man in his unity and integrity who is made in the image of God (Gen. 1:26, 27; 2:7; 9:6). Man is body, and it is not possible to exclude man in this identity from the scope of that which defines his identity, the image of God.[17]

The reformer John Calvin expressed it as follows:

The image of God extends to everything in which the nature of man surpasses that of all other species of animals … And though the primary seat of the divine image was in the mind and the heart, or in the soul and its powers, there was no part even of the body in which some rays of glory did not shine.[18]

Berkhof says that 'We need not look for the image in the material substance of the body; it is found rather in the body as the fit instrument for the self-expression of the soul.'[19] The body and its faculties and the invisible aspects of man are vehicles to demonstrate our likeness to God.

It is the whole man, body and soul, that will be raised at the last day (1 Cor. 15:42). Redemption means the renewal of the whole man. The Christian's *body* is described as the temple of the Holy Spirit (1 Cor. 6:19–20) and we are to glorify God through it.

Let us see how we are to understand this. In Genesis 1 we read, for example, that God spoke and God saw. Other Scriptures refer to the mouth of God (Deut. 8:3; Matt. 4:4) and to His eyes (Ps. 34:15; 1 Peter 3:12). Obviously, these are not physical structures, but our mouths and eyes are made to image those aspects of the Spirit nature of God. So that which God does with His mouth and eyes, we are able to image in our bodies.

Similarly, the Bible speaks of God's hands (Isa. 48:13; 66:2). Our hands reflect what His hand does. No wonder our hands are so wonderful and unique in the creation! When looking at how we image God in our communication, we referred to God writing the laws with His finger (Exod. 31:18; 34:1).

We can find references to other parts of our anatomy which are related to the LORD Himself. Perhaps one aspect that illustrates the principle well is the fact that we are upright. This physical feature reflects God's nature: 'Good and upright is the LORD' (Ps. 25:8). What is true of us physically can also be used to describe us spiritually: '[David] walked before you [God] in faithfulness, in righteousness and in uprightness of heart towards you' (1 Kings 3:6); 'Job ... was blameless and upright' (Job 1:1).

This upright posture is also significant in that we can look upwards to the heavens, a reflection of a spiritual action. We are reminded of the Lord's injunction to 'Look up' (see Luke 21:28). This contrasts with the natural posture of animals, which directs them to the ground.

Being upright has other blessings which might be considered significant, such as having our hands free. This enables us to do things, as in our earlier point about us being creative: we need not only the brains to reason out plans but also hands able to perform the task. Our bodies are a means of displaying God's nature.

Because man was made in the image of God, his body was a suitable vehicle for God who came into this world. Paul often makes the point that Christ was Spirit and flesh (e.g. Phil. 2:5–11). Our Lord was born in 'the likeness of men', just as man had been created in the likeness of God. This echoes Christ's words to His disciples after His resurrection (Luke 24:36–40) and the prologue to John's Gospel (John 1:14). Clearly, Christians are to image the Lord in both spirit and flesh (Rom. 8:29).

We are not free, therefore, to do with our bodies (or our neighbours' bodies) as we wish. We cannot say, 'I have a right to do what I want with my own body.' Christ's taking on a human body at His incarnation underlines how special the body is. We must not cheapen it or degrade it.

The ultimate statement concerning its specialness is the fact that Christ, in glory, retains the human form.

In conclusion, since man is made in the image of God, he is special in God's sight. So:

- Man is to be loved for who he is. Francis Schaeffer expressed it this way: 'All men are our neighbours and we are to love them ... We are to do this on the basis of creation, even if they are not redeemed, for all men have value because they are made in the image of God. Therefore they are to be loved even at great cost.'[20]
- Man's life is to be protected (Gen. 9:6). This affects our attitude to abortion, ethnic cleansing, euthanasia—and even the way we drive our cars!
- Man's reputation is to be protected (James 3:9). To describe a person as anything less than human is contrary to God's will: we are not the cousins of the ape; we are made in the likeness of God. We should not talk of someone who is in a coma as a vegetable. We should not insult people by likening them to animals.
- Man's soul is to be our concern (John 3:16).

That is why this creation message is so important. Francis Schaeffer also commented that if he had only one hour to spend with an unbeliever, he would spend the first fifty-five minutes talking about creation and what it means for humanity to be made in the image of God, and then he would use the last five minutes to explain the way of salvation.[21]

This teaching of man being made in the image of God challenges the way we treat the disadvantaged in society, whether the poor or disabled; it removes any excuse for racism; it assures those who feel isolated or rejected that they are indeed important: God loves them all and individually. And so should we.

Paul encourages us, '... be imitators of God, as beloved children' (Eph.

5:1). This *should* be natural to us as those made in the image of God, but, because of the Fall, it is supernatural, the work of the Holy Spirit.

Biologist Thomas Huxley, when contemplating mankind, commented, 'I know of no study which is so utterly saddening as that of the evolution of humanity ... He is a brute, only more intelligent than other brutes, a blind prey to impulses which as often as not lead him to destruction ... and fill his life with barren toil and battle.'[22] What a difference the creation message makes to our view of mankind! When we contemplate these matters, our reaction should be that of the psalmist when he too thought of how special we are in God's sight: 'O LORD, our Lord, how majestic is your name in all the earth!' (Ps. 8:9). This is a thought that obviously impressed itself on David, as he used it in a prayer: 'Who am I, O Lord GOD ...? ... you are great, O LORD God' (2 Sam. 7:18, 22).

Evolution denigrates the nature of man. Creation puts him in the right relationship with God and the rest of creation.

Notes

1   Quoted in **Fredrick S. Leahy,** *The Hand of God* (Edinburgh: Banner of Truth, 2006), p. 4.

2   **Carl F. H. Henry,** *Christian Personal Ethics* (Grand Rapids, MI: Eerdmans, 1957), p. 89.

3   **Ranald Macaulay** and **Jerram Barrs,** *Christianity with a Human Face* (Leicester: IVP, 1979), p. 14.

4   **A. A. Hoekema,** *Created in God's Image* (Exeter: Paternoster, 1986), p. 67.

5   Since writing this chapter, I have seen that Ranald Macaulay used the same expression, 'theomorphism', back in 2000.

6   **Bruce A. Ware,** *Father, Son and Holy Spirit: Relationships, Roles and Relevance* (Nottingham: Apollos, 2005), p. 58.

7   Ibid. p. 61.

8   *Secrets of the Stone Age,* Channel 4, 2000; available within UK at www.channel4.com (accessed August 2013).

9   **Marc Hauser,** 'What Do Animals Think about Numbers?', in *American Scientist*, March–April 2000; available at http://www.americanscientist.org/issues/num2/what-do-animals-think-about-numbers/5; accessed July 2013.

10 **Charles Darwin,** *Life and Letters of Charles Darwin*, quoted at http://www.goodreads.com/quotes/344554-but-then-arises-the-doubt-can-the-mind-of-man; accessed August 2013.

11 **C. S. Lewis,** *Christian Reflections* (Grand Rapids, MI: Eerdmans, 1975), p. 89.

12 **Arthur Kornberg,** 'The Two Cultures: Chemistry and Biology', in *Biochemistry*, 26/22 (1987), 6888–6891.

13 **N. Chomsky,** *Language and Mind* (San Diego: Harcourt, Brace & World, 1972), p. 97.

14 **Charles Darwin,** 'Religious Belief', in *The Autobiography of Charles Darwin*; available at http://www.update.uu.se/~fbendz/library/cd_relig.htm; accessed July 2013.

15 Quoted in 'Genes, Altruism, and Evolution: Examining the "Urge to Love" in an Evolutionary Sense', 16 April 2003, at http://serendip.brynmawr.edu/, the website of Bryn Mawr College, Pennsylvania; accessed August 2013.

16 **Richard Dawkins,** *The Daily Telegraph*, 31 August 1992 (page not known).

17 **John Murray,** 'Man in the Image of God', in *Collected Writings of John Murray*, vol. 2 (Edinburgh: Banner of Truth, 1977), p. 39.

18 **John Calvin,** *Institutes of the Christian Religion* (Cambridge: James Clarke, 1957), 1.15.3.

19 **Louis Berkhof,** *Systematic Theology* (Edinburgh: Banner of Truth, 1958), p. 205.

20 **Francis A. Schaeffer,** *The Mark of the Christian* (London: Norfolk Press, 1970), p. 10.

21 Cited in **Jerram Barrs,** *Francis Schaeffer: The Man and His Message* (St Louis: Covenant Theological Seminary, 2006), pp. 11–12.

22 **Thomas Henry Huxley,** *Agnosticism*, 24 (1889), 191.

The Fall: the first great catastrophe

D uring a visit to Argentina to speak on 'creation', I was interviewed on the radio. The interviewer was very interested in what I had to say, but asked, 'John, that is all very wonderful. But that is not the world as we see it. What has gone wrong?' It was the difference between Genesis chapters 2 and 4, namely chapter 3. We cannot deal biblically with the nature of evil, God's holiness and so on unless we accept Genesis 3 to be historical and true. The rest of the Bible's teaching on sin and salvation stands or falls with the truth and reality of this passage. If the Fall is not real—not historical—there can be no gospel and no Christianity.

The ultimate statement concerning man's state is found in Genesis 6:5–6: 'The LORD saw that the wickedness of man was great in the earth, and that every intention of the thoughts of his heart was only evil continually. And the LORD was sorry that he had made man on the earth, and it grieved him to his heart.'

We are no better today than Adam. We try to minimize the nature of Adam's sin. Often the LORD's enemies blame Him for His harshness. 'It was only an apple,' they say. We have that attitude to our sin today, too. It was once traditional to dismiss the theft of an apple from someone's garden as 'scrumping'. We reclassify untruths as 'little white lies'.

Aside from the false identity of the fruit, we see from the Genesis 3 account that the sin was much more serious than people realize. It was disobedience, indeed, rebellion. Adam rejected God's authority. In fact, he failed to live up to his own responsibility by not stopping Eve from taking the fruit and then by taking it himself (3:6). They listened to the 'father of lies' (John 8:44) rather than the God of truth. The serpent accused God of lying: 'You will not surely die. For God knows ...' (Gen. 3:4–5).

The serpent tempted them with the offer to be like God (Gen. 3:5)—yet they were so already (1:27). He challenged them not to listen to God but to listen to him. 'Be your own master,' he advised them, but 'Do what I say'. God had said, 'Eat of any tree but one' (2:17), but Satan said, 'Eat of the one tree.' This was thus an invitation to rebellion, to usurp God's authority, and Adam went for it. When God spoke to Adam, He pointed out that Adam had disobeyed Him: 'Have you eaten of the tree of which I commanded you not to eat?' (Gen. 3:11).

The key to the seriousness of this situation is that God is holy and wholly trustworthy (James 1:17–18). He is perfect and man was (and is) disobedient. What happened in Genesis 3 was serious.

Our friends who challenge the historical accuracy of the Genesis account also need to note New Testament references to the Fall. For example, Paul alludes to this event as an illustration of a different problem: 'I am afraid that as the serpent deceived Eve by his cunning, your thoughts will be led astray from a sincere and pure devotion to Christ' (2 Cor. 11:3). Notice how several aspects of the Fall are mentioned here: the serpent, his cunning and the deception of Eve. The truth of the Genesis 3 account is, therefore, critical to the argument. This verse also gives the clue as to the real nature of the Fall: 'your thoughts will be led astray from a sincere and pure devotion to Christ.' That is the key to the severity of the act.

The Fall, as it is fittingly described, was the *first great catastrophe* and it brought down God's judgement. If Genesis 3 is not historical, how do we account for evil and death biblically? To say it is the result of evolution, as does, for example, Richard Dawkins, does not answer the question. Furthermore, if there is no sin, there is no accountability and the message of God's grace is without foundation. But man *is* responsible.

What's gone wrong? The Bible has a big little word: SIN. Genesis 3 is a statement against God's goodness of Genesis 1–2. It was not evolution but revolution. Satan tempted Adam and Eve to 'play God', and they fell for it.

This led to the perversion of creation (Fig. 6). The result is that we judge what is right or wrong by the present worldview rather than the original, created worldview. For example, authority is seen as bad. Yet authority characterizes the relationship within the Trinity, and man was given authority for the good of the woman (and the family)—not to make her a slave or to oppress her. Because authority has been abused since the Fall, we see it as bad, rather than re-establishing it as it was in God's creation plan.

> Work has become labour
> Love has turned to lust
> Carers have become exploiters
> Authority became fear and tyranny
> Health has been marred by sickness
> Spirituality has turned to idolatry
> Righteousness has become hypocrisy
> Life closes in death

Figure 6: The perversion of creation

It is similar with the Sabbath rest. God blessed the Sabbath (Gen. 2:3) and, as Christ pointed out, He did so for man's benefit. Now, as a result of the Fall, we see it as a burden. In fact, of course, we have made it a burden—for example, by abandoning the principle of keeping it special and avoiding unnecessary work. We have effectively made a seven-day working week for many.

Spirituality is despised and seen as an opt-out from reality. It is, in contrast, *the* reality. Man has neglected his spiritual life and to him God says, 'Fool!' (Ps. 14:1; Luke 12:20).

The Fall and broken relationships

The effects of the Fall can be summed up in terms of the relationships which were damaged or destroyed (Fig. 7). In the perfection of Eden, Adam and Eve enjoyed peace with God, with each other and with the world. The catastrophe of Genesis 3:6 tore this apart.

Man and God	man hiding from God
Man and woman	man covering himself from his wife
Man and man	man murdering his brother
Man with himself	his mental torment
Man and nature	thorns and thistles

Figure 7: Broken relationships in the Fall

The devil promised that their eyes would be opened (3:5); they surely were, but in a way he had not disclosed (3:7). These broken relationships were in part the inevitable outcomes of the Fall, though the last one was a specific judgement from God.

Though not the first mentioned chronologically in the passage, the most serious and fundamental was the *broken relationship between the man and his God*. We are told that beforehand they had been living in close harmony. However, after their rebellion, when Adam and Eve 'heard the sound of the LORD God walking in the garden in the cool of the day' (Gen. 3:8), they ran away from Him and hid themselves behind a tree. Can you imagine anything so stupid as thinking you can hide from the almighty and omnipresent God behind a tree? But that is again an effect of sin. No longer were they to walk with Him step by step, talking and sharing with Him, learning from Him of His works. We will see that they were eventually driven out of the garden, from His presence. But, oh, the grace of God! This fellowship that they lost was something that others were to know: 'Enoch walked with God … 300 years' (Gen. 5:24, 22). In His grace, we can do the same today. We can walk with Him and talk with Him. But that anticipates our next chapter.

The first effect that Adam and Eve actually realized was their *broken relationship with each other*, man and wife. Chapter 2 had concluded with the statement that they were both naked and not ashamed by it. Now, their nakedness became a source of embarrassment; as a result, they covered themselves with fig-leaves.

I think we have often missed the significance of this dramatic change. Whatever its extended application for us may be, it is not a matter of public decency but of the intimacy between husband and wife. There had been nothing wrong in their nakedness; it was how God made them and was, therefore, a sinless state. But this embarrassment was a natural result of sin. It marked a loss of trust between them, a loss of openness. They had failed each other. When sin comes between us, intimacy is lost until the relationship is restored.

God did not order them to cover up; sin demanded it. Their sewing aprons of fig-leaves to cover their nakedness was the act that God chose to refer to as an indication of their disobedience (3:11). However, His grace came through again, as He knew that the fig-leaves would soon wilt and the covering be lost, so He made them clothing from animal skins (3:21), an act symbolic of the need to shed blood for the forgiveness of sins.

Furthermore, we see a deep fracture between the man and his wife. He blamed her (Gen. 3:12). The arm that should have been around her for love and protection was now stretched out in accusation. This was unfair, of course (and God didn't let him off the hook), because he was there when Eve was tempted, yet did not use his God-given authority and responsibility to stop her. He said, 'The woman whom you gave to be with me, she gave me fruit of the tree, and I ate' (3:12). 'It's her fault, God. And it's Your fault, too, God.' Aren't we just the same today? We blame others for our misdemeanours.

Then in Genesis 4, we see the *broken relationship between man and man*, specifically between one man and his brother. Much has been said about the cause of this murder. Certainly it was jealousy because God had accepted Abel's sacrifice rather than Cain's. But the Scriptures tell us why God accepted Abel.

Hebrews 11:4 indicates that Abel acted in faith. Later, the writer to the Hebrews refers to the incident by comparing it with the sacrifice of Christ (12:24). It was a blood sacrifice. It was God's determined way. It seems that Cain did the same as his parents: he disobeyed God's instructions. Hatred was, therefore, in his heart and he too was rejected by God. How do we deal with those Hebrews passages if Genesis 4 is not true and historical?

The natural relationships between man and man have been transformed into jealousy and murder. Heterosexual relationships have become marred by homosexual ones.

We see these same effects working out today in our world, sadly even sometimes within churches when God blesses others whom we have dismissed. We miss the blessing because, like Cain, we act against them instead of repenting. The problem of racism which has plagued our world down the centuries is resolved in the creation account (Acts 17:26).

Perhaps we also see the fourth broken relationship in the same passage; we certainly find it throughout Scripture: *the broken relationship with ourselves*. Mental torment plagues so many in society—perhaps all of us at times. We suffer from feelings of inadequacy, of doubt (even doubting God's love for us), of guilt and so on. Francis Schaeffer expressed it this way: 'The basic psychological problem is trying to be what we are not, and trying to carry what we cannot carry. Most of all, the basic problem is not being willing to be the creatures we are before the Creator.'[1]

For man and woman, we see that the image of God has been shattered. Yet even in his sin, man is still in the image of God: 'Whoever sheds the blood of man, by man shall his blood be shed, for God made man in his own image' (Gen. 9:6). It is like looking into a shattered mirror: we can see something of the likeness, but it is distorted.

But there was also a *broken relationship between man and nature*. Man had been given authority over God's world. The world was to be subject to his management. As we have seen, the psalmist cites this as an aspect of his being in the image of God (Ps. 8:6–8). The writer to the Hebrews quotes this psalm but notes that it is no longer the case: 'Now in putting everything in subjection to him, he left nothing outside his control. At present, we do not yet see everything in subjection to him' (Heb. 2:8). As we will see in the next chapter, the writer then goes on to show how our Lord Jesus became like us (without sin), so that He might restore that relationship.

We can imagine (I'm sure correctly) that, as God and Adam walked and talked in the garden, the man asked God about the works He had made. As he looked on the beautiful flowers and birds, for example, he would comment, 'My God made these; isn't He great?' He would ask God how things worked and why He had made the animals and plants the way He did. He would worship his Creator: 'How great You are!'

After the Fall, however, when he worked the ground, pruning the shrubs and so on, he would prick his fingers (Gen. 3:18). His comment now would be, 'How great is my sin!' That is why God cursed the ground: to make us aware of our sin and so come to Him in repentance. Just as the realization of the mess he had got into caused the 'prodigal son' of Luke 15 to come to his senses and return home to his father, so the mess we make and encounter should bring us home in repentance to God.

The creation account presents us with the only explanation of the origin of these relationship troubles. Furthermore, creation is about reconciliation, a renewed relationship. This is clear when God speaks about His people as the 'new creation' (2 Cor. 5:17–18). That is the work in which He rebuilds the relationships which we have broken through our sin and our rebellion.

The Fall and God's judgements

It might seem that we have already been discussing God's judgements. In a sense we have, but those are the inevitable results of our sin. In addition to those, God declared specific judgements (Fig. 8). These, too, are based in this Genesis account which some would reject, yet they are clearly stated there to be a discontinuity in man's history, not an inevitable part, indeed a tool, of evolution. We have here another very direct clash. We have to ask: did God say and do these things or did He not? The truth of Scripture hangs on this.

Judgement on the serpent
  loss of limbs (3:14)
  enmity between the serpent and the woman (3:15)
  ultimate judgement through the woman's offspring (3:15)
Judgement on the woman
  pain in childbirth (3:16a)
  conflict in marriage (3:16b)
Judgement on the man
  painful work (3:17b–19a)
  return to dust (3:19b)
  banishment from the garden of Eden (3:23–24)

Figure 8: God's judgements

It becomes apparent to any Bible student that these judgements are tied to our salvation (see next chapter). The battle between the devil and the seed of the woman meets an end in Christ. The conflict in marriage is overcome as the people of God reflect Christ and His church in their marriages. The judgement on man in his labour will be reflected at the cross and his banishment from the presence of God will be heard in the Saviour's cry from the cross.

The banishment from the garden and so from the presence of God typifies the removal of heaven from the world. It is no longer normal for man to walk with God. This interaction of the two spheres will, of course, be recovered in the new heavens and the new earth.

The reality of the curse on the ground is also reflected in the teaching of the New Testament. Why does nature 'groan' (Rom. 8:20) and await its redemption if there was no curse? Another New Testament statement loses its meaning if Genesis 3 is not historical. How can nature be restored and the curse be removed if there was no Fall?

It is, however, worth pausing to consider the 'return to dust', as this has been an area of conflict for those who abandon the trustworthiness of Scripture. We have to ask whether this is a natural process or God's judgement. Theistic evolutionists see it as the former, since death is the means by which evolution occurs. Indeed, their timescale of billions of years requires death and their concept of our ancestors includes death. The reference to returning to the dust does, of course, reflect man's creation from the dust (Gen. 2:7). If the reference in the creation is symbolic of man's evolution from ape-like ancestors, this judgement must reflect his return to the same.

Yet death is not a part of the 'good' of Genesis 1. God's verdict on human death is plainly stated: 'The last enemy to be destroyed is death' (1 Cor. 15:26).

It is clear from the epistles that this judgement does indeed cover both spiritual death and physical death. We are 'dead in our trespasses' (Eph. 2:5). That happened to Adam on the day he disobeyed God. But this was also the moment when physical death told hold of him. He could not have died physically that day or else there would have been no offspring. As the federal head of the human race, he passed on the verdict of death to all his descendants. Death came to all people, as illustrated in the genealogy of Genesis 5, where 'and he died' is repeatedly continually. Since this was not a necessary statement, having already said how long the person had lived, it must have been included deliberately to emphasize the judgement.

Thus, Adam died spiritually *immediately*; he died physically *ultimately*. This is echoed in the Gospels concerning Christ: He destroyed spiritual death *immediately* and He destroyed physical death *ultimately*.

But we need to remember, too, that we are no different from Adam and we are living under God's judgements. This is mentioned in a very specific way in Romans 1 and is again related to the creation. Paul, by the Holy Spirit, shows that God's eternal power and divine nature are made apparent in the creation around us (v. 20). However, in our folly, we have rejected the Creator, exalting instead the animal world. Nature is not to point us back to a supposed original single cell, but to God. Those who reject the Creator profess themselves to be wise, but God says they are fools (v. 22).

Isn't that a picture of what has happened in evolutionism? This has generated God's anger and so judgement. Romans 1 describes three very specific judgements by God on man.

Firstly, 'God gave them up ... to sexual impurity (v. 24). Secondly, He also 'gave them up to dishonourable passions' (v. 26), which, in the context, is clearly homosexuality. Then, thirdly, He 'gave them up' to depraved minds (v. 28). The two verses that follow describe what is meant by the term. Don't these three judgements reflect the world in which we live today? Creation doctrine is fundamentally important, not only to our spiritual well-being but also to the whole of society. May God have mercy on us.

Romans 1 makes it plain that sinful man suppresses and distorts the revelation of creation. We see this plainly in some of our leading atheists. Do we allow them to determine our approach to Scripture in this (or in any other) matter? As Paul expressed it, 'Claiming to be wise, they became fools, and exchanged the glory of the immortal God for images resembling mortal man and birds and animals and creeping things' (Rom. 1:22–23). A couple of chapters later, he points out the significance of this: '… all have sinned and fall short of the glory of God' (3:23).

The issue of the reality of the Fall has important implications concerning the character of God Himself. If evil had always been present, as implied by evolutionary models, God must be the source of evil. He would not be morally perfect. But God is not the source of evil: 'God cannot be tempted with evil, and he himself tempts no one' (James 1:13). He created man perfect. As the Bible says, the evil around us is the consequence of our sin.

Many of our theistic evolution brethren claim that Adam was not a historical person and so they have to deny that we are by nature sinful. These Christians also deny that physical death is the judgement God imposes, claiming that this judgement is spiritual death alone. So, as we shall see in the next chapter, the divine promise of free grace, and so eternal life, is weakened.

It is significant that in the creation account we find the first record of doubt being cast on the reliability of the Word of God: 'Did God really say …?' (see Gen. 3:1). Does the Bible really say that in six days the Lord created the heavens and the earth (Exod. 20:11; Gen. 2:1–2)? Does the Bible really say that God told Adam that, because of his sin, 'from dust you came and to dust you will return' (see Gen. 3:19)? Does the Bible really say that Christ died for our sins (1 Cor. 15:3)? Does the Bible really say that thorns and thistles are part of the curse of God on the earth for man's sin (Gen. 3:17–18)? Does the Bible really say that the Flood covered the whole earth and destroyed all air-breathing land animals (Gen. 7:19–

23)? Does the Bible really say that 'As it was in the days of Noah, so shall it be when the Son of Man returns' (see Matt. 24:37)?

Evolution rejects the truth of the Fall. Creation recognizes its reality and so is able to present the correct diagnosis, prognosis and remedy.

Note

1 **Francis Schaeffer,** *The Complete Works of Francis Schaeffer*, vol. 3 (Wheaton, IL: Crossway, 1982), p. 329.

God's grace: Christ the Creator and Saviour

Almost a century ago, a non-evangelical minister identified the major problem with evolutionary theory: 'Evolution is now approaching the citadel of our Christian faith. It is affecting Soteriology and Christology.'[1] It seems to me that the problem is still present, even with the rise of the theistic evolutionary position, not least because it falls foul of the biblical record of creation, the Fall, and our salvation as recorded and implied in Genesis.

When man fell into sin and God declared His judgements, His grace shone through once again. Even in that blackness we see His grace and mercy. God announced the coming Redeemer. Addressing the serpent, He said, 'I will put enmity between you and the woman, and between your offspring and her offspring; he shall bruise your head, and you shall bruise his heel' (Gen. 3:15). Furthermore, the New Testament reveals that this plan was made before the creation of the world: '... he chose us in him before the foundation of the world' (Eph. 1:4); 'He was foreknown before the foundation of the world but was made manifest in the last times for the sake of you who through him are believers in God, who raised Him from the dead and gave him glory, so that your faith and hope are in God' (1 Peter 1:20–21).

'Before the foundation of the world.' The creation was not an accident or chance. The Fall was not an incident unforeseen by God. He knew it all and planned our salvation, which was to come through our Lord Jesus Christ, the subject of these references.

Let us be clear that, if the Fall of Genesis 3 was not a historical reality, the gospel is a fraud. We cannot be saved from a judgement that is the result of the evil God Himself created. God is holy and cannot be the originator of evil.

Christ the Creator

In describing the coming of our Lord Jesus, the Scriptures make it plain as to who He was and is: nothing less than the Creator. We find this truth plainly stated in John 1:3: 'All things were made through him, and without him was not anything made that was made'. Again, in Colossians 1:16 we read, 'For by him all things were created, in heaven and on earth, visible and invisible, whether thrones or dominions or rulers or authorities—all things were created through him and for him.' Then in Hebrews 1:2 we read the same truth: '... his Son, ... through whom also he created the world' (see also v. 10).

Did Christ create the world? Everything in it? Or did He just 'throw the switch' and wait to see what evolved? As Creator, He had control over nature and so His miracles, supernatural to us, were natural to Him. For example, we see Him still the turbulent waters of Galilee (Luke 8:24). He who caused the turbulence of the Noahic Flood was able to still the waters of the Jordan as Joshua and the Israelites crossed it, quieten the Mediterranean Sea when Jonah was cast into it (Jonah 1:5) and calm Galilee for the disciples by a word. No problem. 'For he commanded and raised the stormy wind, which lifted up the waves of the sea ... He made the storm be still and the waves of the sea were hushed' (Ps. 107:25, 29).

He who gave life to the figure created from the dust (Gen. 2:7) was able to raise the widow's son (Luke 7:14–15) and His own friend, Lazarus (John 11:43–44). He who caused water to flow from the rock in the wilderness (Exod. 17:6) was able to turn water into wine at Cana (John 2:8–9). After all, it was He who created the grapes, which, fed by water in the soil, generate wine. Suddenly, these things seem perfectly normal actions of the Creator. Write off the early chapters of the Bible, however, and the argument fails.

In Revelation 3:14, He is introduced as 'the beginning of God's creation'. The word translated 'beginning' is *arche* in the Greek. This is the word for planner or designer, as in the English word 'architect'. This is the One we worship and adore.

Christ the Saviour

But when we look again into John 1, Colossians 1 and Hebrews 1 we see something more: Christ is the Saviour. In John 1:12, we are told that it is through Him that we come to God. In Colossians 1:20, Paul says that 'God was pleased ... through him to reconcile to himself all things ... making peace by the blood of his cross'. In Hebrews 1:3, we are told that, 'After making purification for sins, he sat down at the right hand of the Majesty on high', a statement that is reflected in Revelation 5:1, 9. No Christian could or would dispute these references, but we see that they come from the same passages quoted above in which our Lord is declared to be Creator. If we minimize this claim that He is Creator God, we have to ask why we should believe the claim that He is our Saviour to be any more reliable. Christ the Creator is inextricably linked to Christ the Saviour. If the first description is but a picture of the reality, is the second also such?

In the midst of His judgements upon Adam's sin, God told Eve that One to be born through her would be the Saviour (Gen. 3:15). From that point, the devil sought to frustrate God's plan. Abel, her righteous son (Matt. 23:35), was killed by Cain, who is described as having been 'of the evil one' (1 John 3:12). Eve recognized that her next son, Seth, was the one appointed by God (Gen. 4:25). Seth's son, Enosh, was born at a time when 'people began to call upon the name of the LORD' (Gen. 4:26). It was through his line that the Messiah came (Luke 3:23–38). The devil moved in Herod at the Lord's birth to seek to kill Him, but he was frustrated by the LORD's intervention (Matt. 2:13–15). Ultimately, our Lord did die, admittedly at the hands of evil men, but at the direction and according to the plan of the LORD God, and as Saviour (Acts 2:23). God's promise in historical Genesis was fulfilled in historical Acts.

The covenant of grace begins here. The promise to *all nations* was to come through 'Eve ... the mother of all living' (Gen. 3:20). It was fulfilled through Abraham and Israel's line, to whom the international promise was reiterated (Gen. 12:3; 18:18), and was completed in Jesus Christ. Isaiah 59:20 promises the coming of the 'Kinsman-Redeemer'; our Saviour had to be Man in order to redeem us.

This Redeemer, as we have already seen, was the 'offspring' or 'seed' of the woman (Gen. 3:15). He is not described as the offspring of Adam (Gal. 4:4). Is this an implied prediction of the virgin birth (Matt. 1:23; Isa. 7:14)?

The creation account presents the *need for salvation*. We see that man is a sinner; he rebelled against God and is under the death sentence. What is the solution? It is another revolution—but by God, not by evolution. We cannot be consistent evolutionists; we have to bring God into the picture. Any attempt that varies from the Genesis account must fall short of the reality.

But the creation record also demonstrates the *nature of Christ's death*. In the garden of Eden, Adam did *his* will; in another garden, Christ submitted to the Father's will, thereby taking the curse and the judgement of the Fall. Adam failed in a garden and lost contact with God; Christ submitted to the Father in a garden and reconciled us to God. The link between our Lord's redeeming work and the Genesis account goes even deeper (Fig. 9).

> He wore a crown of *thorns*
> He suffered *pain*
> He *sweated* in Gethsemane
> He shared our *nakedness*
> He was *abandoned* by God
> He *died* for our sins
> He died on the *cross* (tree)—
> the place of the curse and the tree of life!

Figure 9: Christ and the cross

The judgement for sin included 'thorns and thistles', so Christ wore a crown of thorns. As a result of his sin and the resultant curse, Adam and his descendants have experienced pain; so, in His crucifixion, the Lord experienced excruciating pain on our behalf. Adam was told that his work in the garden was now to be hard labour causing him to sweat; our Lord Jesus bore that, too, as He prayed in Gethsemane. Adam became embarrassed by his nakedness; our Saviour died naked, taking our shame. Because of his sin, Adam was excluded from the presence of God; Christ also experienced being forsaken by God on our behalf because He bore our sin. Because of his sin, Adam was denied access to the tree of life. Our Lord's death was on a tree: a new tree of life. The faithful and penitent Ephesian Christian was promised food from the tree of life (Rev. 2:7; see also 22:2), a probable allusion to the cross since the unusual word 'tree', *xylon*, is used elsewhere of the 'accursed tree' on which the Lord Jesus died for sinners (Gal. 3:13; 1 Peter 2:24; Acts 5:30; 10:39; 13:29).

There is an important parallel passage to Genesis 3 in 1 Corinthians 15, where verse 26 points out that the Lord's work of salvation will be completed in His final victory over death. This will happen when we are raised to eternal life, never to die again.

There is another link to Christ's work as our Redeemer through Abel: 'Jesus, the mediator of a new covenant, and to the sprinkled blood that speaks a better word than the blood of Abel' (Heb. 12:24). What is the implication if Abel is not a historical figure and his murder is fiction? What, then, happens to the 'better word'? Our Lord Jesus also referred to Abel's murder (Matt. 23:35)—and He can only tell the truth.

The creation account also affects the doctrine of the atonement. Atonement is meaningless if sin is meaningless, and that must be the case if human history is evolutionary rather than biblical. The Scriptures tell us that Christ *died* for our sins, and that He *died* because death is the judgement for sin. That death was physical, not simply spiritual, just as His resurrection was physical. It is very significant that, when Paul was defending the truth of the resurrection of our Lord, he based his argument of proof on the fact that God was Creator (Acts 17:18, 23–31). This same passage demonstrates how important the Genesis doctrine of the creation of man is as a key to his evangelistic message (Acts 17:25–27). These parallels are not coincidental and are lost if the evolutionary explanation for the origins of man and evil are correct.

As we look back over the events described in Genesis 3–4, we see that both chapters contain serious acts of disobedience. However, we see a balance of God's holiness and His love, His judgement and His mercy in each case. Adam's sin brought judgement, including death; God announced the coming of the Saviour. Adam's disobedience brought a sense of shame and embarrassment; God provided animal skins to replace the fig leaves. Cain killed Abel; God provided protection for him and his family (Gen. 4:15). In each case, we have a dark scene of sin and judgement; yet in each case, God shows mercy. Ultimately, this reaches us in our salvation, too.

Then, the creation passage makes sense of *the new creation*. Christ *reconciles* us to God, thereby reversing the effects of Genesis 3. He *restores* in us the image of God: 'And we know that for those who love God all things work together for good, for those who are called according to his purpose. For those whom he foreknew he also predestined to be conformed to the image of his Son, in order that he might be the firstborn among many brothers' (Rom. 8:28–29); '… if anyone is in Christ, he is a new creation. The old has passed away; behold, the new has come' (2 Cor. 5:17).

He makes a new home for us, which, like Eden, has been prepared in advance for us. This is described, for example, in the book of Revelation and has clear resemblances to that original home. Is that to evolve? Why should it be any different from the original in Genesis 1?

The link between the Creator and Redeemer is also made in the Old Testament: 'Thus says the LORD, your Redeemer, who formed you from the womb: "I am the LORD, who made all things, who alone stretched out the heavens, who spread out the earth by myself"' (Isa. 44:24). As Creator and Redeemer, our Lord Jesus becomes the new Head of the restored creation.

Christ the Ruler

Christ is shown to fulfil the command that was given to Adam to have dominion over the created order. In Hebrews 2, as we have seen, we are reminded of what man was intended to be: 'You made him for a little while lower than the angels; you have crowned him with glory and honour, putting everything in subjection under his feet' (Heb. 2:7–8). The writer is quoting the psalmist:

> … what is man that you are mindful of him,
>   and the son of man that you care for him?
> Yet you have made him a little lower than the heavenly beings
>   and crowned him with glory and honour.
> You have given him dominion over the works of your hands;
>   you have put all things under his feet,
> all sheep and oxen,
>   and also the beasts of the field,
> the birds of the heavens, and the fish of the sea,
>   whatever passes along the paths of the seas.   (Ps. 8:4–8)

This, in turn, reflects the Genesis account of our creation and mandate. It cannot have meaning other than in the biblical account.

The writer to the Hebrews then notes the result of the Fall: 'Now in putting everything in subjection to him, he left nothing outside his control. At present, we do not yet see everything in subjection to him' (Heb. 2:8). However, he is able to move on triumphantly:

But we see him who for a little while was made lower than the angels, namely Jesus, crowned with glory and honour because of the suffering of death, so that by the grace of God he might taste death for everyone. For it was fitting that he, for whom and by whom all things exist, in bringing many sons to glory, should make the founder of their salvation perfect through suffering. (vv. 9–10)

Notice that this passage deliberately confirms our Lord as Creator and Saviour. In Ephesians 1:22, we see that this rule is not just over this world but also over the church. This passage and a parallel one, Colossians 1:18, reflect the completeness of the command to Adam to have dominion over everything (Gen. 1:28). Adam was to be fruitful, multiply and fill the earth. The Last Adam has done that and commissions His people now to go out and fill the earth with His disciples: 'All authority in heaven and on earth has been given to me. Go therefore and make disciples of all nations, baptizing them in the name of the Father and of the Son and of the Holy Spirit' (Matt. 28:18–19). The authority that He claims is His by right because of His work of redemption (Phil. 2:9–11) and reminds us of the ultimate fulfilment of the promise to Adam to 'put all things under his feet' (Ps. 8:6).

It is worth noting that the purpose of the book of Hebrews was to show how the historical events and figures of the Old Testament were completed in Christ. If Genesis is not true history, the whole of the author's thesis in Hebrews falls down. We have already seen that Hebrews opens with the identity of Christ as Creator and Saviour. The former title is picked up again in Hebrews 11:3. Those who believe the biblical account of creation are, by implication, part of the gallery of the faithful listed in that chapter.

The New Testament is unambiguous. It makes the first Adam as literal as the last, the new Head of humanity. Romans 5:12–21 and 1 Corinthians 15 are lengthy descriptions of this. Paul emphasizes that through Adam we all die (Rom. 5:12–14). The contrast with the Last

Adam is that in Christ we are made alive. In fact, Paul is quite specific in saying that 'Adam … was a type of the one who was to come'. The use of a 'type' involves the *fulfilment* of the former by the latter. A figment of someone's imagination could not be a type of the real Saviour. Paul makes the same point in 1 Corinthians 15:22. In the second part of that chapter, Paul is very clear:

Thus it is written, 'The first man Adam became a living being'; the last Adam became a life-giving spirit. But it is not the spiritual that is first but the natural, and then the spiritual. The first man was from the earth, a man of dust; the second man is from heaven. As was the man of dust, so also are those who are of the dust, and as is the man of heaven, so also are those who are of heaven. Just as we have borne the image of the man of dust, we shall also bear the image of the man of heaven.　　(1 Cor. 15:45–49)

Again, notice the number of parallels in this passage to the Genesis account. They are not trivial but foundational to our faith.

The message of the creation account and the gospel is that mankind can be restored into God's image (Rom. 8:29). 'Restoration' means a return to what once was. To understand the image, again we must look at the original context, Genesis 1:26. All the positive features we noted in Chapter 4 about the image of God in man were spoilt by sin. God has promised that those who submit to Him in repentance will be restored into His perfect image (1 John 3:2). Yet if we treat the beginning (the Fall) and the end (the Restoration) of salvation history as myth, what do we do with the central point: the work of Christ?

However, we are being made again into the image of His Son: He has not finished His work in us yet. As I close this chapter, I am singing to myself that great hymn from the Rwanda revival, 'Oh, How the Grace of God Amazes Me!' The last verse is:

Come now, the whole of me, eyes, ears and voice.

Join me, creation all, with joyful noise:
Praise Him who broke the chain holding me in sin's domain,
And set me free again. Sing and rejoice![2]

Evolution dismisses the need for salvation. Creation gives us hope of salvation: God can do it!

Notes

1 **J. M. Wilson,** 'The Religious Effect of the Idea of Evolution', in *Evolution in the Light of Modern Knowledge* (London: Blackie & Son, 1925), p. 499.

2 **E. T. Sibomana,** tr. **R. Guillebaud**. Copyright, Church Mission Society Archives.

This world: its purpose and fulfilment

As we have moved through these chapters, we have considered the significance of the early chapters of Genesis for biblical theology. Often, it is emphasized that the creation account is not science but theology. That is right, but it is often expressed for the wrong reason. The account is not science because it is about the miraculous: that which, as we have seen, is natural to God but supernatural to us. One might say that 'science' begins after the sixth day.

In the New Testament historical records (the Gospels and the Acts of the Apostles), we see how the miracles were often a vehicle for the Lord Jesus and His disciples to teach those who witnessed them. So it is in Genesis. Just as the miracles were real in the New Testament and so underlined the truth of Christ's teaching, so it is with the creation account.

For this penultimate chapter we turn to the world itself, created on purpose and for a purpose by our great God. There are no mistakes here. In Job, we see how the events he experienced on earth reflected what was happening in the heavenly places. So it is in the Bible with respect to this world: it is a stage upon which, as we have seen, God shows His sovereign power and nature (Rom. 1:20).

The curtain on the stage is lifted to reveal a unique situation—unique in the whole universe. The garden of Eden has been likened to a temple, and I believe this is right. It is in this garden that God meets with man. Man is, perhaps, serving as a king-priest. When the man sins, that temple is closed and the remainder of the Old Testament prepares, in prophecy and symbolism (e.g. the tabernacle and Solomon's temple), for the coming of Christ, Creator and Saviour. Haggai spoke encouragement to those rebuilding the temple in Jerusalem (Hag. 2:1–9), telling them how God would come to it. John describes God as 'tabernacling' with us (literal reading of John 1:14).

The New Testament then prepares us for the second coming of Christ and the new temple, the 'new Jerusalem', where God's people will meet with Him and worship Him for ever (Rev. 21:3). We see again how the opening chapters of the Bible point to the final ones. Both are God's deliberate acts.

Raising the curtain

So, what do we learn about the earth as it was at creation and as it is now? The curtain rose as God created the world in which we live. The heavenly hosts tell us that the creation was for *God's pleasure*: 'Worthy are you, our Lord and God, to receive glory and honour and power, for you created all things, and by your will they existed and were created' (Rev. 4:11). No wonder He said that it was 'very good' (Gen. 1:31). And we know that God's standards of goodness exclude sin, evil and death (Rev. 21:4).

But we also learn from the creation account that the creation was for *man's benefit*. We have already noted that the LORD was preparing this planet as a home for us. We are, therefore, not surprised to find that it is 'just right' for humans. Some scientists have even described it in terms of the Anthropic Principle, that is, that the world was apparently designed for us. Of course, this also implies that there must be intelligent design.

It is certain that there are a number of physical features of the universe which are so critical that even a very small change in their values would cause the universe to disintegrate. How did they achieve such values? For example, the relationship between the earth and its sun and moon is critical. If the sun were 5% closer or 1% further away, life would be impossible. The number of such 'coincidences' has caused even some sceptics to acknowledge that the earth is probably unique in the universe for supporting life. Did these placements come about by accident through a Big Bang or by the hand of God?

Isaiah says, '... he did not create it empty, he formed it to be inhabited' (Isa. 45:18). This reflects the structure of Genesis 1. Paul tells us that 'God created [the world] to be received with thanksgiving by those who believe and know the truth. For everything created by God is good ...' (1 Tim. 4:3–4).

God created the earth (and, one can argue, the universe) for our benefit. It provides us with food (Gen. 1:29; 9:3; Ezek. 34:29), clothing (Gen. 3:21), medicine for healing (Ezek. 47:12), materials for construction (Hag. 1:4, 8) and wood for making fire (Isa. 44:15). It also provides us with the means for measuring time (Gen. 1:18; Jer. 31:35) and for finding our direction through the world (Num. 21:11; Isa. 45:6). The heavens also give us 'signs' of the weather (Matt. 16:2–3). The prophet Isaiah tells of us using the resources for artwork (Isa. 44:13); we are also encouraged to use them to research the works of God (Ps. 111:2). In addition, the earth gives us assurance of God's continuing care (Gen. 8:22; 9:16).

However, the creation account lays another foundation. Nature is a *witness to God*. Just as a piece of art betrays something of the character of the artist, so nature speaks of the attributes of our Creator. For the psalmist, for example, *the earth speaks* of God's goodness (Ps. 147:9), His authority (Prov. 8:22–29), His eternity (Ps. 90:1–2), His immutability (Ps. 102:25–27), His omnipresence (Jer. 23:24), His transcendency (Ps. 97:9), His trustworthiness (Luke 12:28) and His keeping power (Ps. 121:2). *The heavens declare* God's glory (Ps. 19:1), His immensity (Isa. 40:12; 48:13), His power (Ps. 33:6), His faithfulness (Ps. 36:5), His righteousness (Ps. 97:6), His constancy (Jer. 31:35–36), His infiniteness (2 Chr. 6:18), His mercy (Ps. 103:11) and His wisdom (Ps. 136:5). David sums it up as the whole creation praising its Maker (Ps. 148).

When we consider the biblical statements, we are confounded by the claims of the evolutionists who say that God was not involved in the processes of the world and heavens in which we live. Indeed, as we consider the creation around us, beyond the deformation of it by man, are we not filled with praise? 'How great You are!'

The intermission

Yet we have moved from the beauties of the perfect creation (even though it does still point to our Creator). Sinful man does not honour Him or give thanks to Him, as Paul writes in Romans 1:21. In accordance with the warnings of that passage, we have turned aside from God the Creator and we worship the creature rather than the Creator (1:25). The world is not for us to exploit as we please, but nor is it sacred so that we cannot touch it; it is given to us to use and care for. We hear talk of Mother Nature, Gaia and the trappings of the New Age movement. May God have mercy on us.

While we await the 'final curtain' on this present age, we have the 'creation mandate' to guide us to our duties. We have already touched on various aspects of this in earlier chapters. When the world was in its perfect state, God commanded Adam to tend it. He was to 'work the ground' and 'keep it' (Gen. 2:5, 15). He would till it, prune the shrubs and do whatever else was needed so that it might continue to be pleasant and fruitful. After the Fall, as we have seen, God cursed the ground so that Adam's management became toil. Now he had to compete with weeds and cope with pain. As man repopulated the earth, he spoiled it by his behaviour.

The earth lies defiled
　　under its inhabitants;
for they have transgressed the laws,
　　violated the statutes,

broken the everlasting covenant.
Therefore a curse devours the earth,
    and its inhabitants suffer for their guilt;
therefore the inhabitants of the earth are scorched,
    and few men are left.   (Isa. 24:5–6)

The earth was and is 'defiled', or polluted, by mankind. This speaks of sin ('transgressed the laws'); thus we are responsible for our environmental disasters. We need to repent and remember that 'The earth is the LORD's' (Ps. 24:1). We need to be clear on this repentance, as many and diverse groups of non-Christians are 'sorry' about the environment, but this is not biblical repentance. Calvin de Witt, Director of Au Sable Institute of Environmental Studies, commented, 'If people at an art gallery saw Rembrandt's paintings being destroyed, they would try and prevent the destruction. Similarly, the earth is the canvas of our Lord and Creator and His masterpieces are being destroyed.'[1]

While there are clear principles by which God's people should live in this world, the environment will remain defiled until the 'final curtain' falls. So, what are our responsibilities? Remember that these principles come from the concept of special creation by God and not from an evolutionary model.

Firstly, we consider *man's accountability*. We are called to be stewards, not owners, of the creation. The earth is to be subdued to produce food, clothing, warmth and so on. The thrust of Genesis 2:15, and of the 'creation mandate' that we have been referring to, is preservation. From the very first day (or hours) of his creation, man was given this work to do. It has never been rescinded. Obviously, the nature of our work has increased with time, but ultimately, whether by our individual actions or corporate decisions, God requires us to care for His creation and ensure that it continues to witness to Him. We are accountable for our use or abuse of this world (and, indeed, the cosmos).

We therefore, secondly, need to recognize *man's responsibility*. As we have just said, this is to care for the world, and the LORD gives us clear instructions in a variety of areas. We are to care for the land itself (Lev. 25). Ezekiel underlines this by drawing attention to the fact that God judges the people who ignore His demands on this matter (Ezek. 34:17–20). We must care for domestic animals (Deut. 25:4). The writer of Proverbs says, 'Whoever is righteous has regard for the life of his beast' (Prov. 12:10). Righteousness is practical.

We must also care for the wildlife (Deut. 22:6–7) and must not neglect to care for the needy (Lev. 19:9–10). These are not optional extras. They are not the prerogative of any political party. As God's people (indeed, as part of mankind), we all have a responsibility to take these issues seriously and do all within our power to meet the LORD's commands.

Following from this is *man's management* of the environment God has loaned to us. As we recognize these responsibilities, we have to consider how we manage them. One clear example in Scripture is the concept of *rest*. We have seen previously how God rested from His work of creation (that is, He had completed it) and marked this by establishing a special day of the week to commemorate it. This was given to us as a model for managing our own lives and the lives of those who depend on us. We also noted that this day of rest was to be given to our working animals. This is surely not only a command to be obeyed but an example of good husbandry. Such animals will serve us better on the other days if they have a Sabbath rest of their own.

The Lord makes the same point to us about our management of the land:

If you walk in my statutes and observe my commandments and do them, then I will give you your rains in their season, and the land shall yield its increase, and the trees of the field shall yield their fruit … Then the land shall enjoy its Sabbaths as long as it lies desolate, while you are in your enemies' land; then the land shall rest, and enjoy its

Sabbaths. As long as it lies desolate it shall have rest, the rest that it did not have on your Sabbaths when you were dwelling in it.   (Lev. 26:3–4, 34–35)

Studies have shown that the effect of such a rest for the land has a dramatic effect on its yield of crops.

God has, therefore, given us the means to fulfil His promises to provide for our needs. Firstly, there is enough food to feed everyone sufficiently. The reason why so many go hungry is because of poor distribution, greed and politics. Secondly, we have the means to increase crop yields. God created the plants (and animals) with the ability to adapt naturally or be bred for yield, resistance to disease, to suit varying soil and climate conditions and so on. God has given us the resources; it is not a matter of chance or luck as to whether there is sufficient. A report from the United Nations' Food and Agriculture Organization concludes that the long-term food outlook for developing countries is good. While the world population is expected to reach eight billion by 2030, growth in global agriculture should be more than sufficient to meet world demand.

One example of how we may legitimately consider improving our food production is through GM (Genetically Modified) crops. We have the ability, but do we have sufficient knowledge and wisdom? In nature, genes are transferred between plant types, but this transfer is clearly controlled (due to God's all-wise creation!). Can we control such a process and carry it out safely? Research is one thing, but the ability to manage at a genetic level may be questioned. However, we do recognize that God has given us the ability to do these things; we must prayerfully consider the risks as well as the values.

An interesting, and apparently successful, project based on the creation approach is known as Farming God's Way (FGW).[2] It is being employed in a number of countries and has increased crop yields significantly. The Bible is not unscientific.

We are endowed with authority to manage and care for the natural order, both fauna and flora. The authority is evident in Genesis 1:28. This and other verses indicate environmental management. The word 'subdue' in Genesis 1:28 has often been misunderstood; Löning and Zenger show this to be an unhelpful translation of the Hebrew and related Semitic words.[3] A better translation would convey the meaning of to 'guide, lead, command'. It expresses the need for man to control nature for the benefit of the whole of creation. 'Subdue' cannot mean 'overcoming its wildness', as God made creation good. Rather, it refers to the productive ordering of the earth to yield its riches and accomplish God's purposes for it.[4]

There are many specific related issues that are relevant for the Christian, but they must be discussed elsewhere. I have sought to uncover the biblical principles—and, as we see, they have their foundation in the biblical account of creation and the Fall.

The environment speaks of God's work and causes us to worship. It also speaks of our sin as we see the effects of the Fall. In addition, it reminds us of our responsibility towards God. God cares about His creation; do we? The creationist protects the environment because it contains wonder, awe and real value.

The final curtain

But, as wonderful as this created world is, it will not last for ever. The curtain will fall and a new creation will be revealed (Rev. 21:1). Everything will disappear from this creation, except mankind. This reminds us of the Flood, except that on that occasion God spared a selection of animals as well in order to repopulate the earth. Peter relates these two events:

For they deliberately overlook this fact, that the heavens existed long ago, and the earth was formed out of water and through water by the word of God, and that by means of these the world that then existed was deluged with water and perished. But by the same word the heavens and earth that now exist are stored up for fire, being kept until the day of judgement and destruction of the ungodly.   (2 Peter 3:5–7)

According to Paul (Rom. 8:20–21), the curse of Genesis 3:17–19 also points to the end times. Even here we see the grace and mercy of our God.

A new heaven and earth will be created, but man will continue. The very term 'new *creation*' implies the original *creation*. When we compare Genesis 1–2 and Revelation 21–22 we see a number of parallels. If we are committed to an evolutionary interpretation of the former passage, are we to see the new creation as an evolutionary utopia? Revelation 21 says that there will be no tears, death, mourning or pain. What is the significance of this 'redemption' if there was no Fall?

In the perfection of Genesis 1–2 we see that heaven, God's home, was a spiritual place encompassing the created, material universe so that God and man had direct fellowship. Sin then caused a rift (Gen. 3) and so God and heaven were 'withdrawn'. Thereafter, the Trinity visited man on occasions. When we turn to Revelation, we see that heaven and the new earth are again in fellowship, hence the perfect communion of Eden will be restored. Man will once again walk with his God (Gen. 3:8) and will have no need to hide from Him.

Of course, while God's people look forward to those times, we shudder to think of the judgement that awaits the godless, those who have rejected our God, Creator and Saviour. Our Lord Jesus, who spoke plainly about those times, referred back to the chapters in Genesis which are dismissed as being, at best, figurative and lacking reality: 'Just as it was in the days of Noah, so will it be in the days of the Son of Man. They were eating and drinking and marrying and being given in marriage, until the day when Noah entered the ark, and the flood came and destroyed them all' (Luke 17:26–27).

Many dismiss the reality of the Flood account. No wonder that, even among evangelicals, we find those who dispute the reality of eternal judgement. In Jude 17–19, the predictions of our Lord and His apostles are contrasted with the scoffers of the final days.

The link between these events is so tight in Scripture that we must conclude that, if the Flood was not global, neither will the final destruction be global. Yet the biblical record clearly states that the Flood was indeed a global judgement. Some have disputed the extent of the destruction, but, for the Bible-believer, there can be little question. It is difficult to conceive how God could have made it clearer than He has done: 'I will blot out man ... from the face of the land, man and animals and creeping things and birds of the heavens' (6:7); 'I have determined to make an end of all flesh ... I will destroy them with the earth' (6:13). Genesis 7 emphasizes this: '*all* the high mountains under the *whole* heaven were covered' (7:19, emphasis added); '*all* flesh died ... *all* swarming creatures ... *all* mankind' (7:21, emphasis added); '*Everything* ... died' (7:22, emphasis added).

If the Flood did not occur, Christ's words would imply that His return will not occur either. The New Testament emphasis is also on the suddenness and unexpected nature of the Flood and so of the 'day of the Lord'. The Lord underlines this Himself in Matthew 24:36–44. It is interesting to notice how even creationists can miss this significance in the Lord's words. The three passages referring to the Flood in the New Testament (Matt. 24:36–44; Luke 17:26–27; 2 Peter 3:4–7) contain ten comments on the suddenness of its coming Flood and the suddenness of the future judgement. As Moses recorded, 'On the very same day ...' that God shut the door of the ark (Gen. 7:13, 16), the Flood came. In His 'Sermon on the Mount', our Lord warned of those who will be excluded from the eternal bliss because they are not right with God. Similarly, He told the parable of the bridesmaids who were locked out at the wedding because they were not ready (Matt. 25:10). Comparison with modern writings on the Flood reveals an absence of this New Testament emphasis on its suddenness and thus of the need to be ready for that great day.

The Scriptures again emphasize God's sovereignty in this. It was He who brought the Flood (Gen. 6:17), who shut the door (7:16), who sent the rain (7:4), who destroyed all life outside the ark (7:4) and who sent the wind that caused the waters to subside (8:1). To reject the biblical account of the global Flood is to doubt the power of God, to neglect the warning to be ready for the final judgement and to impugn the character of God. This issue of the final judgement and its relationship to the days of Noah was summed up well by the late J. Montgomery Boice: 'The proof of the final judgment is the fact that God has already judged the world once in the great Flood of Noah … The final judgment is no less certain than the former one.'[5]

The Lord goes on in Luke 17:28–30 to link the 'final curtain' to the days of Lot and the judgement of Sodom and Gomorrah, as does Jude in Jude 7. I don't know of any evangelicals who dispute that event, but our Lord relates the days of Noah and Lot to 'the day when the Son of Man is revealed'.

In Genesis 3:15, we read of God's ultimate judgement on the devil. This was achieved through the cross, but its completion will be seen only at the final judgement. The devil is appropriately described as the serpent in Revelation 20:2; he will be cast into the fire prepared for him and his angels (Rev. 20:10). This is a fulfilment of Genesis 3—but only if Genesis 3 is true history.

As we have seen, Peter underlines the same parallel between the events of the creation, the Flood and the final judgement. But he also links these events to the grace of God: just as God saved Noah and Lot and their families, so there will be deliverance for all who repent (2 Peter 3:9). 'But according to his promise we are waiting for new heavens and a new earth in which righteousness dwells' (3:13).

As we look back to the global catastrophe, the Flood, we see the ark that God provided for 'righteous Noah' (Gen. 6:9; 2 Peter 2:5). Similarly, in Christ, we shall be saved from that greater and final catastrophe. If the

Scriptures are incorrect concerning the saving of only those in the ark, who will be saved at the Lord's coming?

In Chapter 2, we noted that both the Old Testament and the New Testament open with miraculous events that defy scientific reasoning. Both Testaments close with God's people looking for the coming of Christ, the first and second comings respectively. Both events are marked by unbelief. When Christ returns, will He find faith on the earth (Luke 18:8)? Yes, He will—but, as in the days of Noah, it will be found among the few. Faith is taking God at His Word (Heb. 11:1–3).

Evolution casts doubt on the promise of the new heaven and the new earth. The creation account is used by the Lord to assure His followers that the promise is true.

Notes

1 **Calvin De Witt,** 'Praising Rembrandt but Despising His Paintings: Stewardship of God's Creation', lecture at Calvin College, Grand Rapids, Michigan, 7 January 1997.

2 Farming God's Way at www.farming-gods-way.org.

3 **Karl Löning** and **Erich Zenger,** *To Begin With, God Created* (Collegeville, MN: The Liturgical Press, 2000), pp. 109–113.

4 **J. MacArthur,** *The MacArthur Bible Commentary* (Nashville: Nelson, 2005), p. 11.

5 **James Montgomery Boice,** *Psalms*, vol. 1 (Grand Rapids, MI: Baker, 1994), p. 88.

Chapter 8

Conclusion

It would be easy to read this book and assess it on the basis of its effectiveness in countering the attack on the historicity of Adam and Eve. I trust that it will indeed be helpful to that end. However, as I have studied and written these words, they have excited me and caused me to praise God. I trust that this book has had the same effect on you, the reader, whether you agree or disagree with my thesis.

To conclude, the Genesis account ...
- shows that God acted sovereignly
- shows that mankind was God's purpose and is special
- shows that the Fall spoilt God's creation
- is fundamental to our salvation and so eternal life
- foreshadows the 'new heavens and new earth'

Creation doctrine is fundamentally anti-evolution because creation accepts the integrity of our Lord Jesus and His apostles; evolution esteems scientific thinking above the Word of God. In addition, evolution cannot explain man as man, nor sin, nor salvation and so on.

I therefore believe that we cannot claim to be evangelical *and* believe in molecules-to-man evolution. The two positions are biblically incompatible. Creation and evolution are concerned with *different relationships*: in whose image are we? Is man related to the chimp or to God? They have *different paradigms* as a basis for life: self-preservation versus self-sacrifice. Then there are *different links*: are we linked to the apes through 'Lucy' (the nickname given to our supposed ape ancestor) or to God through Jesus Christ? Consequently, there are also *different destinies*: have we come from slime and are we going to rot, or have we come from the hands of God and are we heading towards glory?

The following comment is, perhaps, a salutary message to Christians who dismiss the Bible account. Dr Jerry Coyne is a well-known evolutionary biologist from the University of Chicago and this is what he said on a recent BBC programme:

Evolution is unique amongst the sciences because it strikes people in the solar plexus of their faith directly. It strikes them at the idea that they are specially created by God, because evolution says you're not; it says that there's no special purpose for your life because it's a naturalistic philosophy; we have no more extrinsic purpose than a squirrel or an armadillo. And it says that morality does not come from God; it is an evolved phenomenon. And those are three things that are really hard for humans to accept, particularly if they come from a religious tradition.[1]

God has revealed Himself in nature *but* this is not sufficient for salvation. Nature speaks of God and spoilt nature speaks of our sin. However, creation shows man to be accountable to God and creation is a cause for worship.

A prisoner sent the following comment to Revd Dave Branon, published in *Our Daily Bread* reading notes: 'I came to the point in my life where I finally accepted the fact that God is real and the Creator of everything. I grew tired of trying to do things my way. When I started humbling myself and accepting God's word, I found the answer.'[2]

In the book of Job we read, 'Then Job answered the Lord and said: "Behold, I am of small account; what shall I answer you? I lay my hand on my mouth. I have spoken once, and I will not answer; twice, but I will proceed no further"' (Job 40:3–5). This was Job's response to God's 'creation sermon'. What is ours?

There is an encouraging comment in Hebrews 11. As is well known, this is a chapter in which God lists the 'heroes of faith', people who through their faith have pleased God and who are, therefore, recorded by Him throughout time. But have you ever noticed who comes first in this passage? 'By faith we understand that the universe was created by the word of God, so that what is seen was not made out of things that are visible' (Heb. 11:3). Creationists may be mocked, insulted as being unintelligent and even dismissed from their jobs as scientists (as quite a number have been), but that 'we' puts them in God's gallery of those who please Him because of their faith in Him and His Word. As Peter says, 'In this you rejoice, though now for a little while, if necessary, you have been grieved by various trials ...' (1 Peter 1:6).

In eternity, we will join with the heavenly ones, praising God: 'Worthy are you, our Lord and God, to receive glory and honour and power, for you created all things, and by your will they existed and were created' (Rev. 4:11). Amen.

Notes

1 **Andrew Maxwell,** *Conspiracy Road Trip: Creationism*, BBC, October 2012.

2 **Dave Branon,** 'My Way?', in *Our Daily Bread*, 30 April 2012.

The days of creation[1]

One subject creationists are often asked about is the nature of the days in Genesis 1. Did God really say, '… in six days the LORD made heaven and earth, the sea, and all that is in them, and rested on the seventh day'?

It is often argued that we 'know' that the creation days were longer than the present twenty-four-hour days. Such bold claims, however, need justification, and it is the purpose of this appendix to explore these claims. I seek to demonstrate that this assumption is invalidated by Scripture and unnecessary in science.

What does the Bible claim?

Christians who are concerned to be subject to the Bible naturally want to follow the Bible rather than any man-made ideas, however clever and interesting the latter may be. So let's go back to the Bible.

We read in Genesis 1 of a series of days in which God created the heavens and the earth and then filled them. In each case, the days are enumerated (the first day, the second, the third, etc.) and are delineated by 'there was evening and there was morning'. Elsewhere in the Bible, whenever the Hebrew word for day, *yôm*, is used (359 times in total) with the ordinal (first, second, etc.), it clearly means a normal day.

The debate about the length of the 'day' is sometimes one of willing ignorance. The word 'day' is used in three ways by the LORD in the creation account: twice in Genesis 1:5 for the period of daylight and for the evening/morning cycle, and then in a general way for the time of creation in 2:4. However, in each case the precise meaning is clear. There is an interesting parallel in a clearly historical passage, Numbers 7, which records the tabernacle offerings made on 'the first day' (v. 12), 'the second day' (v. 18) and so on, through to the more general use of 'the day' (v. 84).

An unbiased reader would therefore interpret the days of Genesis 1 as meaning real or natural days. We understand a day to be a period of twenty-four hours. Though there may have been some variation in this period of time during history, that would not be significant in affecting our understanding of this wording. The period of time called a day is the time of the rotation of the earth about its axis.

Virtually every Hebrew scholar who has examined the subject admits that *it is the clear intention of the writer* to convey the idea of creation being completed in six periods of twenty-four hours.[2] To avoid any misunderstanding, we are not saying that God took twenty-four hours to complete each stage of creation. The acts of creation may well have been instantaneous, but each group of activity described was limited to this discrete period of time.

This has an interesting consequence. The terms 'day', 'month' and 'year' have clear astronomical meanings,[3] but where does the concept of the 'week' come from? It is derived from the Genesis account of creation alone *and* is defined by 'six days of activity and one of rest'. This is reiterated in the fourth commandment (Exod. 20:11).

What did God mean?

Many who would agree with our response to the first question would go on to say, 'Ah yes, but God …' The gist of their comments would be that the passage cannot be interpreted in a literal sense; it is simply a convenient way of communicating the idea. Does this approach hold water?

Many claim that Genesis 1 (and through to chapter 11) is not written as historical narrative but is in another form. Varied claims have been made: poetry, metaphor, myth, parable, story, analogy,[4] allegory and so on. With so many suggestions, it clearly does not conform to any one of these well-known Hebrew or Near Eastern literary forms. As Prof. Gerhard F. Hasel puts it, 'The obvious consensus is that there is no consensus on the literary genre of Genesis 1.'[5] It would seem, therefore, that these are all cases of special pleading in order not to face the obvious fact that it is written as, and reads as, a straight historical narrative. Prof. Gordon McConville has noted that 'There are indeed metaphorical uses of "day" in the Old Testament ... But metaphorical uses of any word are always based, and depend, on the literal meaning ... You cannot erect a scientific theory on a metaphor.'[6]

For whatever reason, the non-historical approach implies that God could not explain the real facts to man in a way that would be intelligible to him. Surely this cannot be a serious suggestion! If I can describe the concept of creation over a long period of time to a child (and I could), then God, the perfect Communicator, would have no problem. Why should God use this misleading imagery? Let's face it, if this claim is true, God has misled His people over many ages. I think not.

Further, it undermines the testimony of our Lord Jesus. When He was challenged about His behaviour on the Sabbath, the Jewish leaders referred Him back to the law. In His response, He did not challenge the law, but actually referred them back to the purpose of the Sabbath (Matt. 12:1–12). Our Lord never hesitated to challenge the validity of the Pharisees' interpretation of the law on other occasions, so He is unlikely to have ignored any misunderstanding of the detail of the Sabbath law.

Why do we want any other meaning?

It is important to ask why we would want to interpret the days of Genesis 1 as being other than real days. I presume it is not because we think God cannot create the universe in six days. Then again, it is not because the biblical text requires some other meaning.

The usual answer to this question involves a statement along the lines of 'Because modern science demands it'. Of course, *science* does not require anything. It is a body of observable facts and a process of research. From that, *scientists* develop interpretations and theories to explain the observations. A Geiger counter will give a reading, but it is the scientist who interprets it and explains what the reading implies.

The basic argument is that scientists have shown through the geological column that the earth is very old and so the great ages demonstrated through dating the rocks in the column must be equivalent to the days of Genesis 1. The geological column is the theoretical correlation of the different rock formations around the world. Though it does not occur anywhere in this complete form, geologists can relate different strata in the different regions to give what they interpret to be the earth's history. It incorporates many fossil remains and the strata are given ages of tens and hundreds of millions of years. So, it is argued by theistic evolutionists, this time span has to be found in Genesis 1.

This is the fundamental error of the day-age theory, that is, the theory that the six days represent six extended periods of time. However, the geological column has *nothing* to do with Genesis 1. An alternative interpretation of the geological column can be found elsewhere, but for the purposes of this study it is sufficient to emphasize the non-equivalence of the creation account and the geological column. Once this perceived link is broken, there is no reason to distort Scripture and the apparent meaning of the days in Genesis 1.

This non-equivalence is demonstrated by comparing the two systems. Genesis 1 is about the creation of what is good—indeed 'very good' (Gen. 1:31). It is about beauty and order. It is about that which gives our God pleasure (Rev. 4:11). It is about harmony. On the other hand, the rocks and their fossils speak of death, destruction, agony and conflict.[7] Whatever the geological column has to say about age, it has no relation to Genesis 1 and creation. *If* millions of years have to be found, they are not to be located within the creation week of Genesis 1 and so there is no need to make the days mean anything other than normal days.

The argument from 2 Peter 3:8

Some point to other texts as their warrant for reinterpreting the passage. An example is 2 Peter 3:8. Aside from the fact that the passage does not refer to Genesis 1 but, rather, to the Flood narrative in Genesis 7–8, it would prove too much. Do those who support such a position wish to equate a day with a thousand years? No, with millions. But what about the rest of the text? It says that a thousand years is equivalent to a day. So a 'day' in Genesis 1 would be equal (according to that part of the verse) to a fraction of a second. Of course, what this verse is saying very plainly is that God is not governed by time. He can do anything He wishes without any time constraint. The question, so far as Genesis 1 is concerned, is not 'What was He able to do?' but 'What did He claim to do?'

It is important to appreciate another important matter with respect to God's creation activity: it was *miraculous*, so taking it beyond the realm of scientific investigation. Genesis 1 is not describing normal cosmological, biological, chemical or physical processes. Further, the Bible tells us that His creation work is *finished, completed* (Gen. 2:2–3). We cannot see God creating now. We are living within and under His providence.

Conclusion

If we want to turn to scientific evidence which supports the normal day time frame, we can find it in such biological aspects as *symbiosis*, the mutual dependence of one species on another. One cannot survive without the other for extended periods of time. This observation is made throughout the biological world. One *could* propose their parallel evolution, but that is clearly not what Scripture describes. If we are to accept the biblical revelation on special creation, we must accept the consequence of the need for a short time span between the creative acts.

If we are to take the Bible account seriously, then, we must recognize that the days of Genesis 1 are normal days, in other words, the period of the rotation of the earth about its axis, defined by 'evening and ... morning'. There is no scriptural reason for believing otherwise. There is no relevant scientific need to reinterpret God's revelation. And for the evangelical Christian, it is the Scriptures, rather than the thoughts of scientists (or even theologians), that are definitive.

Notes

1 This article was originally written for, and distributed by, the Biblical Creation Society. It was also published as a chapter in **John F. Ashton** (ed.), *In Six Days* (Sydney: New Holland, 1999). It has been modified and updated for the purposes of this book.

2 This was acknowledged by Professor James Barr in a letter to David C. C. Watson, 23 April 1984: 'So far as I know, there is no professor of Hebrew or Old Testament ... who does not believe that the writer(s) of Genesis 1–11 intended to convey to their readers the ideas that ... creation took place in six days which were the same as the days of 24 hours we now experience.' Quoted in **K. Ham, A. Snelling** and **C. Wieland,** *The Answers Book* (Green Forest, AR: Master Books, 1991), p. 90.

3 The *day* is the period of rotation of the earth on its axis. The *month* is defined by the period of the moon's orbit around the earth. The *year* is described by the time of the earth's orbit around the sun.

4 **Meredith G. Kline,** in 'Space and Time in the Genesis Cosmogony' (1996), has argued from analogy ('replication relationship') that the 'days' were part of the heavenly 'register' ('And God said ...') and the results in the lower, earthly register ('and it was done'). The allocation of the 'day' to the upper register is arbitrary and the author fails to deal adequately, if at all, with the 'evening and morning' framework. At http://www.asa3.org/ASA/PSCF/1996/PSCF3-96Kline.html; accessed July 2013.

5 Gerhard F. Hasel, in *Origins* (GeoScience Research Institute), 21/1 (1994), 5–38.

6 **J. G. McConville,** 'Interpreting Genesis 1–11', in **Nigel M. de S. Cameron,** *In the Beginning ... A Symposium on the Bible and Creation* (Glasgow: Biblical Creation Society, 1980), pp. 5–17.

7 In addition, the order of the creation acts does not correlate with the evolutionary mode. For

example, the sun is created on the third day (not the first outcome), the fish are made on the fifth day (they were not an earlier form of earthly life); the birds are also created on the fifth day—before the reptiles.

The history of mankind[1]

In this book, our concern has been with the theological issues and, in general, we have avoided scientific aspects of the creation–evolution debate. However, it does seem appropriate to give some guidance on the matter of the biblical history of mankind and how that relates to fossil findings.

Human beings are specified scientifically by the Latin prefix *Homo*. Though quite a variety have been identified among the sparse fossil record of human beings, we can simplify our discussion by concentrating on three: *Homo erectus* (upright man), *Homo neanderthalensis* (Neanderthal Man) and *Homo sapiens* (intelligent man—that is, us).

The relationship has been variously considered: a linear development in the sequence as listed or the former two as branches from the third by, perhaps, mutation or environmental pressures (Figs 10 (a) and (b)).

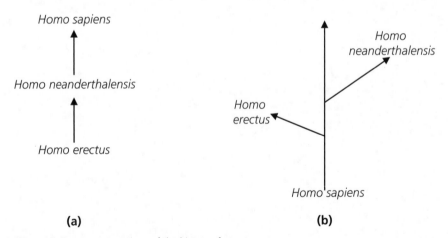

(a) (b)

Figure 10: Two representations of the history of man

Anthropologically, we can relate them to the Stone Ages:

Homo erectus	—	Old Stone Age
Homo neanderthalensis	—	Middle Stone Age
Homo sapiens	—	New Stone Age

The archaeological terms based on the Stone Ages run parallel to the Ice Age stages (Pleistocene), as shown in Figure 11.

How, then, do we relate these to the biblical account, specifically to Adam and Noah?

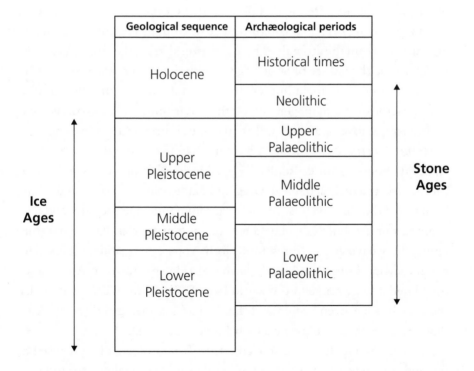

Figure 11: Relationship of the archaeological and geological terminology

True humans

Firstly, we need to establish the fact that the archaeological evidence demonstrates that these Stone Age people were 'true humans' and not glorified apes; in no way is one inferior to the other. This has been well established over recent years but is worth reviewing here to dispel any doubts. One anthropologist, Dr Richard Rudgley, summed up the situation well by opening a TV series, *Secrets of the Stone Age*, with the statement, 'Stone Age man was as intelligent as we are.'[2] We will see that they appear to show all the faculties that can be determined from archaeological remains that confirm this.

Genesis 2:7 indicates that there was no pre-Adamic human: God's breath brought him life; he had none until that moment. We have seen that man, having been made in the image of God, has features that make him distinct from the animals. There are several areas that we can look at to determine the nature of Stone Age mankind in order to assess his true human distinctives, including creativity, intelligence, communication, self-consciousness, management of the environment, industriousness, relationships, love, worship, ability to make choices and a conscience.

Homo erectus, Old Stone Age man, has been found to have had elaborate housing, for example. He lived in small family units and cared for the sick and disabled. He devised and made beautiful tools, and it has been noted that his javelins were very aerodynamic. He used fire and left examples of art which displayed manual and artistic skills. He had the ability to weave plant fibres into cloth, ropes, nets and baskets. He produced fine fabrics and made headgear. He spread from Africa and populated a huge range of the world from Spain in the west to China in the east. It is has even been noted that he had sea-faring skills. It is clear that he passes the test of being a truly human individual.[3]

In 2009, archaeologists discovered that *Homo erectus* had devised a method of making a very strong adhesive, equivalent to today's 'superglue', which the researchers had difficulty reproducing. They said that their research gave them a 'new respect for these prehistorical people'.[4]

Homo neanderthalensis, Middle Stone Age man, commonly known as Neanderthal Man, has an equally impressive record. He made a range of ornaments such as rings, necklaces and beads. He was skilled in the production of tools and musical instruments. He was both a farmer and a hunter, and also fished using harpoons. He also left significant works of art. He practised medicine, surgery and dentistry, even using anaesthetics and antiseptics. He demonstrated a sense of the spiritual, as shown by his care for the dead in their burial. He was clearly able to speak. He was physically powerful. As indicated by his name, he was first found in the Neander Valley in Germany, at the edge of the ice fields of the Ice Age. Since then he has been found in similar locations across Europe.

Early pictures of him minimized the human aspects of this man, but a reconstruction from his remains in the Rheinische Landesmuseum gives a very different picture. Dressed in a suit, he is almost indistinguishable from ourselves. One palaeoanthropologist commented, 'To be Neanderthal is a distinct way of being human.'[5] Again, we would be unwise to consider him as anything but true man. Indeed, there is good evidence that he interbred with other *Homo* species, such as *Homo sapiens*.

Homo sapiens is 'thinking man'. As shown in Figure 11, the end of the Ice Age was marked by the appearance of New Stone Age man, Neolithic man. The change in the climate aided the development of the advancing culture. He was no cleverer than his predecessors; he simply had new opportunities to exploit the skills already apparent in our description of them.

In building construction, we move from home construction to megalithic structures such as Stonehenge in England, which also demonstrates advanced skills in mathematics, engineering, astronomy, trading, transport, management and so on. Large towns have been found (e.g. Çatalhöjük in Anatolia). There is clear evidence of religious beliefs. He knew of, and used, drugs and practised a range of surgery. He extended the range of musical instruments. We detect, too, examples not only of language, but also of writing. Grime's Graves in England give evidence of a sophisticated mining industry. A number of Neolithic wells have been found.

We have been fortunate in having a very good example of such a man. He is variously known as the Ice Man or Özti man, so named after the place in which he was found. There have been a number of books written on him following extensive amounts of research (still ongoing). This Ice Man was discovered by walkers in the Ötztal Alps on the Austrian-Italian border in 1991. He was beginning to appear in the melting ice. He was well preserved and his possessions were intact. It has been estimated that he died about four to five thousand years ago, at the end of the Ice Age. He had essentially been in deep freeze all this time. He was 5 ft 3 in. tall and weighed 8 stone, had brown eyes and hair, and was about forty-five years old at death. He suffered from diseases such as arteriosclerosis and Lyme disease. Analysis of his stomach contents showed that a day or two before he died he ate a meal of goat and plants, but his last meal was venison and cereal. He was killed by an arrow (the head was found in his shoulder) which severed an artery. This was probably the result of an intra-tribal rivalry and followed a hand-to-hand fight, but unusually for those communities, he appears to have been buried and then his remains abandoned. Remarkably, with his DNA having been analysed, it has been possible to relate him to named living relatives.[6]

As mentioned, his possessions were found intact and researchers have studied these carefully. He had well-stitched clothing and shoes which were appropriate for the climatic conditions. He was equipped with bow and arrows and carried tools such as a flint knife and a bronze axe (note the use of bronze in the Stone Age). On his belt he had a pouch which contained materials for lighting a fire. In his pocket were plants which are well-known for their antibiotic properties. His body had some strange marks on it, but a Japanese researcher qualified in acupuncture identified them as the sites that he would use for treating his arthritis.[7]

Indeed, he and we are very much of the same *Homo* stock. It is helpful to compare the advances in our culture in the last century with those between the various Stone Age cultures. We are no cleverer than our grandparents (or even our great-grandparents); we just have new opportunities to develop our culture.

We conclude, therefore, that *Homo erectus* and *Homo neanderthalensis* were, like ourselves, the *Homo sapiens*, true humans. They differed only in phenotypic features, that is, characteristics which can be due to genetic variations, environmental selection and so on. There is no evidence that *Homo sapiens* are superior. The question then becomes: how do we all relate to the biblical account of man?

The biblical origins of man

Biblically, we start with Adam, whom we can describe as *Homo creatus*, 'created man'; we can then relate him to the above *Homo* descriptions.

Adam was created by God as a perfect and complete person, reflecting his Maker. His skills are clearly outlined, even if only briefly. Not only could he speak, but he had a complete vocabulary, being able to name the animals. This required intelligence. He was able to communicate with God, which undoubtedly means that he could worship, too. It is apparent from the mandate given to him that he was able to manage the environment—tilling the ground, for example. He clearly had the power to make choices, as demonstrated by his failure in Genesis 3. The same chapter also shows that he had a conscience. When he sinned, he had a need to make clothing.

The range of skills in Adam and his descendants is also apparent from Genesis 4: farming (v. 2, both animals and arable), building cities (v. 17), constructing and playing musical instruments (v. 21) and working with metals (v. 22). When we come to the account of Noah, we see that he had vineyards and made wine (9:20).

The Fall obviously made life harder and sin affected man's choices, leading then (as now) to bad decisions (as with Cain and Lamech—4:8, 23). We see failures, too, with Noah and his family (9:21). However, though the image of God in man was distorted (as when we behold ourselves in a shattered mirror), he was still as true a man as *Homo creatus*.

There were clearly anatomical variations between humans. For example, before the Flood there were the *Nephilim* (6:4). And what was distinctive about the 'mark on Cain' (Gen. 4:15)? Post-Flood, we read of giants (*Anakim*, Deut. 2:10) and of men with six fingers and six toes on each hand and foot respectively (2 Sam. 21:20).

The Flood resulted from man's sin (Gen. 6 indicates that the causes were illegitimate relationships and violence). After the Flood, man returned to his sinful ways, but the LORD made it clear that man was still in His image (9:6). Though the physical resources available to people immediately after the Flood had been destroyed, they still had the knowledge necessary to begin again. Additionally, of course, Noah and his family had the experiences from before that destruction to relaunch the technologies of those days.

From that point on, we move to the cultures of modern societies, as the LORD displaced them from Shinar to occupy the whole world (Gen. 11). It is clear to anyone who follows the archaeological news that, though the range of technologies available to us has increased dramatically in the last century or so, 'ancient man' was no less intelligent and able than us. One only has to look at the detail of a monument such as Stonehenge to appreciate that.

But this leaves us with questions as to how to relate the biblical record to the biological classification of mankind.

Relating to the scientific data

It is beyond the brief of this book to explore all the science behind the origins of man. Fortunately, this has been covered elsewhere and we can just select items that we need in order to consider the issues that concern us.

Basically, our distinctive physical characteristics are produced in *our genes*. These are stretches of the chromosomes that generate proteins that are, in turn, taken up in our biochemical processes and so determine such basic matters as the colour of our skin and of our eyes, or the nature of our hair—whether it is naturally straight or curly and so on. (We are well aware nowadays that the genes are not the total story. Other stretches of the chromosomes which have been discounted in the past are now known to have very important roles in cell activity. Also we recognize that there are factors in the cells beyond the genes which control the activity of the genes; this is called *epigenetics*. For our purposes here, we can ignore these important and fascinating aspects.)

When we consider eye colour, for example, we find that there are several genes controlling this aspect, giving, in simple terms, brown or blue eyes. Which colour we have depends on which of the genes we inherit from our parents. So, different children of the same parents can have different eye colour. As we go through all the factors managed in this way, we can see that there are multiple possible combinations, so that our children are usually distinguishable in a few if not many ways.

Some years ago, Prof. F. J. Ayala calculated the possibilities across the world population. He estimated that around 6.7% of our genes show these sorts of variations. Translated into the number of possible combinations, he reckoned that one couple would have to have 10^{2017} offspring before they could be certain of having two who were identical. That number is so big that it exceeds by a very long way the number of anything we can begin to imagine. There are not even that many atoms in the universe.

That is the genetic potential in our cells. Sometimes I am asked how we could get the different 'races' from one couple, Adam and Eve. Not difficult! Again, keeping the answer simple, we can consider skin colour, which is usually used to mark out different people groups. (Remember, though, that skin colour is only skin deep and underneath we are the same.) It is reasonable to assume that Adam and Eve were a middle-brown colour. This is because the genes for skin colour are based on those that generate white skin and those that generate black skin. If child number 1 inherited only the 'white skin' genes from each parent, he or she would be white. Similarly, if child 2 inherited the 'dark skin' genes, he or she would be black-skinned. A mixture of the two would give the same colour as the parents.

Over the generations, of course, the range of options for all the different genetic results would increase markedly. It is worth noting, too, that in the early generations after the creation and after the Flood, there would have been 'inbreeding' among close relatives, such as cousins, which can give significant variations to the general pattern. As family groups dispersed after the Flood, this sort of isolation effect would have continued.

In the light of this, questions have been posed by some critics of 'special creation' as to how long ago our original parents must have lived to generate the extent of the variation we find in the world today. It is usually argued that it would have required millions of years. Some interesting work on this subject was published in 2012 by a team from the University of Washington. They studied the extent of the genetic variation in the current population and estimated that the maximum likely time required to reach this state would be just over 5,000 years.[8] So the biblical account is not scientifically unreasonable.

But how do we relate biblical history to the fossils? Because, for example, in the UK we can go down to the Dorset coast and readily collect fossils, we might assume that fossils are abundant and that we therefore have an extensive record of life in the past. However, the vast proportion of these fossils relate to aquatic creatures. As we move up through the rock strata, ultimately reaching mammals and man, the numbers drop dramatically. In fact, human fossils are quite rare. It has been commented by some palaeontologists that the number of such fossils relating to early man can be packed into a car boot. That may be an exaggeration, but it illustrates the problem. The fossils found are very fragmentary. Most useful are skulls—though these are normally incomplete—and almost complete skeletons are very rare.

In order to understand the pattern, it is useful to consider a simplified diagram of the type of distribution found in an animal family and relate it to the biblical history (Fig. 12). There would have been variation before the Flood, but one form (possibly the original species) would have survived the Flood by being taken into the ark. After the Flood, more variation (not necessarily the same) would have occurred. Also shown in the figure is cross-fertilization between species of the same genus or family.

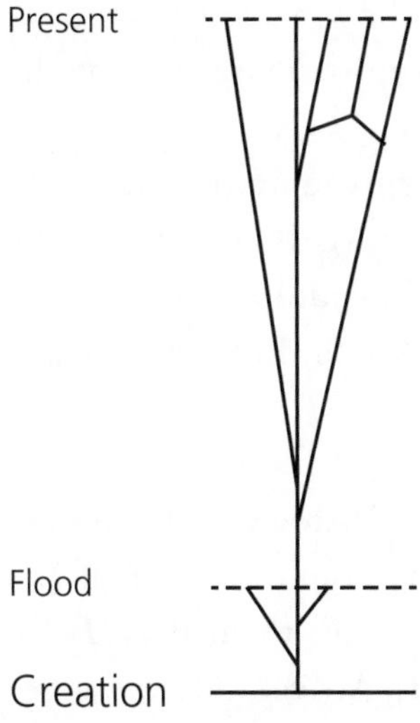

At the Flood, only one pair of each animal kind was taken on to the ark (seven pairs of the 'clean' animals), so the diversity was immediately reduced, as the land air-breathing animals and birds were totally destroyed. However, the genetic potential would have enabled further diversity post-Flood. This reduction at the Flood is described as a 'bottleneck' since some of the creation genetic versatility would have been lost from the gene pool. In the creation model, we cannot be sure of the original created kinds.

Present

Flood

Creation

Figure 12: A simplified diagram showing the development of animal species from a 'founder' member in a biblical scenario

The same principle must have applied to the human kind. Basically, we can say that the line of Cain and Adam's other offspring (except Shem) would have been lost and only a small proportion of Seth's line would have survived. But we must remember that Noah's sons had three wives, who could have carried genetic traits from other lines. So, post-Flood man would have begun with at least 50% of Noah's genes (through his sons), the balance being made up from the genetic make-up of Noah's daughters-in-law.

There is no trace of pre-Flood man because God 'blotted out' all trace of him (Gen. 6:13; 7:23). So, Stone Age man (i.e. Ice Age man) was also post-Flood. Therefore, we have no knowledge of how *Homo creatus* compared with *Homo erectus*, *Homo neanderthalensis* or *Homo sapiens*. We would not expect dramatic differences, since we continue in the same 'kind' and in God's image.

How can we relate this information? The following three diagrams build up an overall picture which gives an approximate idea of the distribution of the various *Homo* species.

Figure 13(a) shows how *Homo erectus* was spread across the world during the early and middle Ice Age times. (The Ice Age is described as the Pleistocene.) They were initially located in the Middle East and East Africa, then gradually spread more widely in Africa, Europe and East Asia.

As we noted earlier, *Homo neanderthalensis* was found later and in Europe (Fig. 13(b)). By the time of the Upper Pleistocene, the human fossils are widely dispersed, initially involving some mixture of the *Homo* types, but eventually the dominant form across them all is *Homo sapiens* (Fig. 13(c)), firstly in eastern and southern Africa.

The dispersion in figure 13(a) would presumably be related to that at the time of Babel (Gen. 11:9). Relating the Ice Age to the biblical history, we note that the Ice Age finished before the rise of the cities. This began after the dispersion (Gen. 10:10), so we conclude that, since Abraham

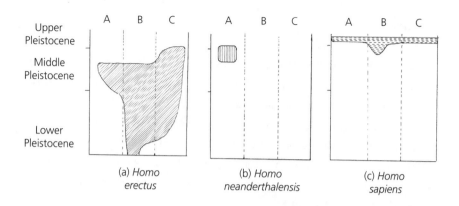

Figure 13: A schematic representation of the appearance of various *Homo* types by time and region based on fossil finds (Key to regions: A: Europe/West Asia; B: Africa/Middle East; C: East Asia)[9]

came from a city and moved into other urban areas (Gen. 11:31), he must have been post-Ice Age and so presumably *Homo sapiens*. If this reconstruction is valid, he was not identical to *Homo erectus* or to *Homo neanderthalensis*, though all these forms were truly human, the differences being in genetic traits.

Please note that, in referring to the various forms of 'true humans' (*Homo creatus, Homo erectus, Homo neanderthalensis* and *Homo sapiens*), I am emphasizing that each of these forms (whether the unidentifiable created man or the discovered fossil men) is a true human. Some early fossil finds consist only of footprints. Though evolutionists will name them otherwise in order to fit them into their scenario, creationists recognize them as those of true humans. In this latter situation the tendency has been to call them *Homo sapiens*, indicating that we have little reason to believe they differed significantly from ourselves. Indeed, I do not see any *significant* difference between these various forms and only retain the terminology in recognition of the fact that physical changes have occurred over time.

Appendix 2

Notes

1 I have been developing some of these thoughts for some time, but I wish to acknowledge my appreciation of a recent paper by Andrew Snelling (of Answers in Genesis) which helped to consolidate them. I would add that my thoughts do, of course, reflect the present state of our knowledge in the areas covered, especially in the matter of human fossils and our understanding of their relationship to the biblical record. While the biblical record is unchanging, our scientific studies are continually under development and some modification may be appropriate in the future, but I suggest that the approach employed here is a suitable model to cope with that eventuality.

2 Channel 4, 2000.

3 **Richard Rudgley,** *Lost Civilisations of the Stone Age* (London: Century, 1998).

4 **L. Wadley, T. Hodgskiss** and **M. Grant,** *Proceedings of the National Academy of Sciences,* 106/19 (2009).

5 **Antonio Rosas,** National Museum of Natural Sciences, Madrid, quoted in 'Neanderthals at Home', 19 April 2013 at http://creationresearch.net/; accessed August 2013.

6 'Our Cousin the Iceman', in *Your Family History,* Spring 2012, p. 12.

7 **L. Dorfer, M. Moser, K. Spindler** et al., '5200-Year-Old Acupuncture in Central Europe?', in *Science,* 282/5387 (1998), 239.

8 **J. Tennessen** et al., 'Evolution and Functional Impact of Rare Variation from Deep Sequencing of Human Exomes', in *Science,* 337/6090 (2012), 64–69.

9 Based on a figure in **Andrew Snelling** and **Mike Matthews,** 'Finding a Home for Cavemen: When Did Cavemen Live?', in *Answers,* April–June 2012, pp. 51–55. Used with permission.

The range of books covering the creation–evolution debate is extensive. The following is a selection of those which tackle the biblical aspects of the issues in part or wholly. Inevitably, even this is not an exhaustive list!

Anderson, David, *Creation or Evolution: Why We Must Choose* (Littlethorpe: J6D Publications, 2008)

Batten, Don, and **Sarfati, Jonathan,** *15 Reasons to Take Genesis as History* (Brisbane: Creation Ministries International, 2006)

Cameron, Nigel M. de S., *Evolution and the Authority of the Bible* (Exeter: Paternoster, 1983) [Unfortunately, this book is out of print, but it is worth picking up a copy if you can find it!]

Fields, Weston W., *Unformed and Unfilled: A Critique of the Gap Theory* (Collinsville, IL: Burgener Enterprises, 1976)

Kelly, Douglas F., *Creation and Change: Genesis 1:1–2:4 in the Light of Changing Scientific Paradigms* (Fearn: Christian Focus, 1997)

Kulikovsky, Andrew S., *Creation, Fall, Restoration: A Biblical Theology of Creation* (Fearn: Christian Focus, 2009)

MacArthur, John, *The Battle for the Beginning: Creation, Evolution, and the Bible* (Nashville, TN: W Publishing Group, 2001)

McIntosh, Andy, *Genesis for Today: The Relevance of the Creation/Evolution Debate to Today's Society* (4th edn.; Leominster: Day One, 2006)

Mortenson, Terry, and **Ury, Thane H.,** *Coming to Grips with Genesis: Biblical Authority and the Age of the Earth* (Green Forest, AZ: Master Books, 2008)

Nevin, Norman C. (ed.), *Should Christians Embrace Evolution? Biblical and Scientific Responses* (Nottingham: InterVarsity Press, 2009)

Peet, J. H. John, *In the Beginning God Created …* (London: Grace Publications, 1994)

Schaeffer, Francis A., *Genesis in Space and Time: The Flow of Biblical History* (London: Hodder & Stoughton, 1972)

Tyler, David J., *Creation: Chance or Design?* (Darlington: Evangelical Press, 2003)

An extensive range of books covering the scientific aspects of the subject has been published by various creation organizations and evangelical publishers. A good starting point would be the CreationPoints series published by Day One Publications.

About Day One:

Day One's threefold commitment:

- To be faithful to the Bible, God's inerrant, infallible Word;
- To be relevant to our modern generation;
- To be excellent in our publication standards.

I continue to be thankful for the publications of Day One. They are biblical; they have sound theology; and they are relative to the issues at hand. The material is condensed and manageable while, at the same time, being complete—a challenging balance to find. We are happy in our ministry to make use of these excellent publications.

JOHN MACARTHUR, PASTOR-TEACHER, GRACE COMMUNITY CHURCH, CALIFORNIA

It is a great encouragement to see Day One making such excellent progress. Their publications are always biblical, accessible and attractively produced, with no compromise on quality. Long may their progress continue and increase!

JOHN BLANCHARD, AUTHOR, EVANGELIST AND APOLOGIST

Visit our website for more information and to request a free catalogue of our books.

www.dayone.co.uk

In God's image
The divine origins of humans

STUART BURGESS

32 PP.

978–1–84625–100–9

Humans have great physical, mental and spiritual abilities that are far beyond what is needed for survival. This 'over-design' provides compelling evidence that man was specially created as a spiritual being. This booklet describes the following unique characteristics of humans:

- Unique upright structure
- Unique skilful hands
- Unique fine skin
- Unique facial expressions
- Unique language and speech
- Unique childhood
- Unique marriage and birth
- Unique brain
- Unique beauty
- Unique genome
- Unique spirituality

The booklet also discusses the origin of man and the purpose of human life from a biblical perspective.

Stuart Burgess has taught engineering design at leading UK universities. He has also carried out spacecraft design for the European Space Agency. In 1989 he received a Design Council Prize for engineering design presented by the Minister of State for Trade and Industry. In 1993 he received the Turners Gold Medal for engineering design presented by the Vice Chancellor of City University.